TAKE IT
FROM HERE

TAKE IT FROM HERE

How to Get from Where You Are to Where You Want to Be

Dr. Sonya Friedman

with C. B. deSwaan

KENSINGTON BOOKS
http://www.kensingtonbooks.com

I dedicate this book to my family, who have supported me through thick and thin while always maintaining their own identity and opinions. They've always challenged me, thereby assuring my ongoing growth. I am grateful.

KENSINGTON BOOKS are published by

Kensington Publishing Corp.
850 Third Avenue
New York, NY 10022

Library of Congress Card Catalogue Number: 2003108435
ISBN 0-7582-0490-6

First Printing: January 2004
10   9   8   7   6   5   4   3   2   1

Printed in the United States of America

Contents

Acknowledgments

No project comes to completion alone. This one was guided and supported by Richard Curtis, my agent, who showed a profound belief in me and my work even when things looked dark. I am grateful for his encouragement and integrity.

The work itself would never have gotten to the printed page if it weren't for my co-writer, Connie deSwaan. This book reunited me with the person who better than anyone else has taken my ideas and helped me translate them so that they were focused and clear.

Last, I'd like to thank my friends who once again gave so generously of themselves by providing their real-life experiences to be used by the reader as examples of life's struggles and triumphs.

To all, a deeply meant thank you.

INTRODUCTION

In 1983 I wrote *Men Are Just Desserts*—which would become a million-seller landmark book for women—followed by the best-selling *Smart Cookies Don't Crumble*. Both were very personal guides. In them, I wanted to answer the intimate, if confusing, questions on every woman's mind at that politically sensitive crossroads where women were discovering what feminism really meant to them on a personal level. Most of all, I wanted to help women create the kind of lives that mattered to them. It would be the end of living by default or duty.

Since the mid-1980s, I've worked in the media, all the while maintaining my private practice. I'm still in the business of helping women—and because I'm a psychologist, they tell me what concerns them at the deepest level. This part of my life is important to me: the truth of their private and professional lives unfolds in my office in a raw and often uncensored way. It means a lot to me that I can, and I have, made a difference for them.

Then, since I give so many speeches all over America, I hear from women at every stage of life. Listening to them is not unlike listening to my patients. And what they say *amazes* me:

- Whatever city they live in, and no matter where they are in life, many women feel as if they've wound up in the wrong place, with the wrong partner, in the wrong job, and living out the wrong, if not predictable, fate!
- While they feel that *something* is missing, they can't define what that something is, or where to find it, or understand why it's lacking in their lives.

This *is* amazing.

There's a line of traditional wisdom that says, in effect, just because the world is a mess doesn't mean you have to become a mess or give in to the messes to get by. When you've grown up, you *can* clear the path and connect with that missing "something." I know it can happen because I've seen it happen again and again.

I've seen the world change and women change with it.

As young women in the 1950s, my friends and I had our roles in life pretty much laid out for us. We were to go to high school, maybe college, but hopefully not graduate without an "M.R.S." degree. Sexually, we did everything *but!* We were supposed to be virgins at marriage, or at least act innocent. If we worked after marriage, it was only as financial helpmates for husbands just getting started in their careers. Then, at least nine months after marriage and not before, we were to become full-time wives and mothers. The idea of voluntarily having a child out of wedlock or living with a man before marriage was spoken about in hushed tones—such liberties hadn't been made acceptable by any stretch of the imagination, except on the fringes of society. In those days, an out-of-wedlock child was considered illegitimate and condemned. Now the focus has changed and when we talk of a single-parent family few people blink.

Most of my friends from those days got divorced. No one figured out that the girl you were at twenty, the average age of marriage at the time, was not the woman you would turn into ten years later. There was no expectation that time and experience might change who you were and what you wanted. I remember my husband saying to me on our eighth anniversary, "You're not the girl I married!" My initial reaction was to fear that I was no longer acceptable, and I became quite upset. Upon reflection, I soon realized that he was right. I was no longer a submissive, breathless little girl who needed him in the same room to feel complete. I was a woman now, with her own opinions—not all of them mirroring his. While I still wanted to be acceptable to him, in truth, I knew I had become a lot more acceptable to me.

Today, it's all different. My practice consists of women who are twenty years old and up, and have so many more choices and opportunities than I and the girls I grew up with had. Their expectations are nothing like those we had. Yet, from what I've heard from women all over the country, I know many women are stuck in a kind of extended adolescence.

Women already have a potent capacity to figure out who they are and what is right for them. However, many do otherwise. Why?

THE REASON FOR THIS BOOK

With all the accepted social allowances for choice and control, women still don't know how to create a balance between intimate relationships, family ties, ethical and moral behavior, and professional achievement. That the juggling act is making women crazed is an understatement. Depression and anxiety are now as common as dental cavities—as is taking medication to calm down, perk up, or sleep. For some women who don't want to grow up, attempting to stay girls with no responsibility or obligations have unwanted consequences: a life alone. In some cases, women have taken on the male characteristics that women used to complain about: devotion to a job rather than to a relationship or the family, aggressive pursuit of sexual partners in and/or out of a relationship, and fear of commitment.

Today, relationships are difficult to define. As a result, women every day deal with edgy live-in relationships, multiple divorces, single parenthood, intensive career paths, massive role confusion, and generational drift. Marriage is often replaced by first living together; in some cities there are more babies born outside marriage than in it.

Twenty- and thirty-year-olds fear growing up and thus put off the developmental tasks of *adulthood*. Forty-year-olds live as they did a decade earlier, hoping their youthful dreams will come true. Women in their forties can suddenly panic and feel desperate to marry and have children. Fifty-year-olds start looking over their shoulders, fearing that the young turks are mobilizing and ready to overtake them at work. At home, they wonder how much of their intimate lives they've sacrificed for a job that may not be worth the effort.

Since women have so many choices, we can no longer blame men, mothers, or corporate machinery for limitations or being where we are. What have women lost or overlooked along the way to self-realization? My research says it is the definition of fulfillment and of being *a fulfilled, adult woman*. The power of being a woman is not only about exploring talents and abilities in the workplace, but about growing up, *civilizing* men and society, being standard bearers, raising daughters who respect themselves and who are not sexually active at fourteen years old, and sons who are not greedily materialistic or brutal—as well as allowing ourselves to find satisfaction in life, whatever that may mean for each one of us.

⁓

Your life is the sum of everything you've said yes and no to so far. This is true of all of us, and there's no changing it—but your history need not be your future. Whether it's about realizing a dream, pursuing a loving relationship no matter what your age, or finally cutting loose from a relative, friend, or group of people who are bad influences on you and keep you down, *Take It from Here* will help you figure out what went wrong and how to make it right.

This is the book that will answer two key questions that will make the difference:

- *What are you seeking?* For most women, the answer is satisfaction or happiness, but they still can't define exactly what it would be.
- *Why haven't you been fulfilled; or, if you have known and lost fulfillment, how can you get it again?*

This book will show you how to become an *adult*, thereby making it possible to define yourself as more than your relationships. It will include your autonomy, your sense of competence, your belief in what love is and where it lies, and, of course, how to understand happiness and capture fulfillment. When you're an adult, you can make your own cake, and eat it, too. But understand that there's no cake without the calories. As a grown-up, you'll know that there are choices to be made and a consequence to everything.

⁓

Take It from Here will motivate you to use your good sense, sensitivity, and smarts to make life go right again! The title was inspired by something I used to hear my uncle Jack say. He was a genius at appreciating life and being resourceful and responsible. My uncle Jack greatly valued where he had come from *and* where he was. He'd awaken every morning and say, "Thank you God, I'll take it from here"—that is, he was grateful that God got him through the night, but he knew that what he accomplished during the day was up to him. Uncle Jack was the kind of man who could face any event and any disaster, and as the expression goes, he'd pray to God, but he'd keep rowing toward land.

This is a big part of my message to you in this book. *Take It from Here* suggests that no matter where you come from—and if that background has held you back—you can let go of it and start living *from here*, now. Only you can get to where you want to be and, like my uncle, have something to be thankful for every day.

Life changes whether or not you want it to. Life is meant to move forward. Allow yourself to ripen, to grow, to mature, to become a fully adult person. There may be some pain in growth, but there's even more adversity and pain when you stunt that growth. Life is really all that you've got, and appreciating it makes a difference.

I hope this book helps you to clarify what your underlying needs are and why they haven't been fulfilled and shows you that you can:

- Feel gratitude that you have made it to this point and take responsibility for what comes next.
- Finally answer the question you've been asking yourself: "What's stopping me from making changes, and what do I need to do?" so that you can determine what is your underlying need.
- Trust in your courage to make life better *now*. This courage provides emotional and spiritual ballast.
- Make peace with all your experiences, and work through those that still cause pain.

- Learn the steps to psychological healing through a new understanding of forgiveness—whether it's forgiving yourself, being forgiven by others, or forgiving others.
- Feel passionate about your life and the relationships you forge.
- Know that mistakes don't break your inner spirit. Rather, mistakes teach resiliency, contribute experience, and give you the kick to get up and start over!
- Understand that you don't live in isolation. What you do and how you live has an effect on others. Doing something with your life is also a decision about improving your community and making an investment in the next generation.
- Know that the pursuit of your own courage, maturity, and wisdom to make life right isn't a solemn quest, but a joyful journey.

The best advice I can give you is to become self-aware. With that awareness, you can shift with change, adapt, and find fulfillment. You'll be able to "take it from here" for the best of times, for the time of your life.

MOVING THROUGH LIFE WITHOUT STALLING

Life Has an "I" in It

"I can't stand it anymore!"

It wasn't only the mid-September heat wave that brought three women to tell me they'd *had it* in pretty much the same words. Within a few days' time, three very different women, grappling with largely different problems, all hit a boiling point. They'd reached the limits of frustration with how their lives were going.

This is what happened to them:

• Amy, a smart, attractive paralegal in her early thirties, has taken on a *Sex and the City* veneer of slick sexual sophistication. Emotionally, Amy says she yearns for a stable relationship with a man she can count on. In reality, she is aggressively pursuing Vic, who's not sure of his feelings for her, and wants to cut back on seeing her to only once a week. Amy cannot accept his terms. Because she fears the breakup is imminent, she has doubled her efforts at persuading him he can't live without her. She pushes; Vic backs away. She tries to seduce him; he doesn't call back. Hence, Amy's breaking point has come, and she says, "I can't take it any longer. I'm calling Vic for a showdown. How many messages do I need to leave him?"

• Nancy is a forty-year-old married, former operating-room nurse with three small children, supported by her husband, and feeling lost in the role of suburban motherhood. Nancy married when she was thirty-one; by the age of thirty-six she had three children, born a little more than a year apart, and she's since devoted herself to a traditional life. Her children are very demanding, and she willingly provides for their needs—but she is increasingly conflicted about *who needs whom*. Does she need them more than they need her?

Nancy fears that by the time the kids are in school full-time and more self-sufficient, it will be too late for her to go back to work and *fit in*. "I can't stand my kids always being on me for something," she told me, "and I can't bear the feeling that I can't live without them needing me. I'm even thinking of having another baby when my youngest goes to school. It gives me a sense of purpose to my life."

• Marcie, in her late twenties, recently separated from her husband of five years. Marcie is a highly functioning realist and hardworking woman who's had a meteoric rise in the telecommunications business. Her husband Ed lost a steady but uninspiring sales job when his company went out of business three years ago. He's been unable to find a day job to his liking and instead earns what money he can in the work that he most loves: playing drums in a band that only works weekends.

Marcie thinks he's wasting his time. To satisfy her pressure to bring in income, he started driving a cab a few days a week while trying to sell the songs he composes. Since Ed earns a fraction of her income, he fails to meet one of Marcie's criteria for a good husband: he must be able to at least pull his own financial weight. Since Ed doesn't, Marcie resents him. What further fuels her anger is that Ed enjoys the upscale life Marcie provides for both of them, and instead of showing his appreciation, he insults her because she's the success that he is not. In addition to being an "inadequate provider," Ed will not have sex with her anymore. Predictably, Marcie and Ed's quarrels almost always focus on money and *who does more*. "I was understanding to a point," she said, "but I've had it. Why can't he understand my side of the money problem?"

To a psychologist, "I can't stand it anymore!" are fighting words. They mean you can no longer avoid what's going wrong in your life and need to start doing something about it. It doesn't matter what you "can't stand," just that you get to the next step: understanding that old patterns and habits aren't working anymore and something's got to change.

These women had little about their lives in common, yet they eventually wound up sharing the same goal: They wanted to know who they really are, how they managed to get to this point, and how to end the sense of loss of complete self and make a better life.

FINDING THE "I" IN YOUR LIFE

If the unsaid and underlying question these three women are asking is, "How did I let this happen to me?" the answer may be, "Because I never allowed myself to know who I really am." This can be a tough truth for many people to face: If you don't like where you are in life, there comes a point when you must give up the part of you that's keeping you back. Then you can become the person you've always wanted to be—the "I" that makes up your individuality. No one else can find that "I" in your life and nourish it but you. That "I" is your identity.

To say that *life has an "I" in it* creates a picture. With the word *life*, three letters other than "I" are needed to form the totality of its meaning. For you, that "I" means that you are the central character in your life, but that others play important supportive roles. Therefore, you cannot go through life thinking only of yourself without it having a devastating effect on others, just as you cannot go through life only doing for others without that having a devastating effect on yourself. When you understand the totality of your life and your responsibility for it, everything changes.

Having an "I" in your life reflects knowing your standards and values, the soul of who you are. Standards tell you who you are, what you're willing to compromise to get what you want, what you've done for expediency, whether or not you can stand up to a fight, how you move along through big and small changes, and how you create great joy and spontaneity in your life.

Most of all, you need to be an *integrated person*. You may have separate facets of your personality, and they may appear at different times, but the integrated you is an example of a *realized* self. A realized self has kinetic energy and a developmental quality that keeps it growing. You can keep working on realizing your self all your life, always defining who you are along the way. When you define who you are, you grow up and ease out of childhood and adolescence into an age of renewal and wisdom. It will take some work. Your world changes only by changing yourself, not the others around you.

If we look at the "I" in the lives of the three women who opened this chapter, we find them at various stages of life, not yet fully realized selves. Each one is confused about who she is at a crisis point. There's Amy, in her thirties, who wants to believe she controls relationships with sex, even an uncommitted relationship, but she doesn't control anything. There are the two slightly frantic women, Nancy and Marcie, who are both overwhelmed, one at the age of forty and the other in her late twenties. One is distraught because she cannot let go of her unrealistic expectations about marriage and the other because she cannot let her children go and face herself.

These women are at a crossroads, not the end of the line—at a turning point in their identity. There's a common feeling among women of all ages that everything's changed, yet it's still the same. If that's true for you, too, then this is the place to start defining "I." By defining what matters, you can move toward it. What matters? The simple truth is that *you* control what you think, what you say, how you feel, and how you behave. Only you can create the true portrait of your life, with color, texture, feeling, spontaneity, joy, and order. Only you can make this truth come alive. This takes courage, but it's the only way to be true to yourself and fight any destructive forces that attempt to divert you from your course.

You can begin to build confidence when you learn that what went wrong can go right:

• For Amy, pursuing a man who is uncommitted is a matter of finding someone to end her loneliness. Relationships aren't about discovering who she is in a couple, because few of the men she chooses have the potential to be a partner. Each man has something wrong for her. Yet, these are the men she invites into her life. What about Amy? Is *she* a potential partner? What does she need to examine about her own identity and work on? Right now, she's sad, self-pitying, and finds rejection "intolerable" by another man who is unavailable and, most likely, not right for her.

It's not easy to accept these cruel truths in life, like rejection in love. Amy has a chance to change who comes into her life. First of all, she has to give up her destructive patterns with men in which she holds on tight, pursues when the man backs off, makes him feel guilty, and hopes that keeps him in for the long run. Amy hopes that guilt will turn into love.

Should she believe this guy could have a change of heart about her? He has been telling her he's not ready for a commitment, not that he wants to end the relationship. For Amy, having an "I" in her life would mean she decides how she wants the relationship to go and then moves in that direction. If they break up, she will need to cope with it. If the man wants them to continue dating each other while dating others as well, she will have to deal with that decision, too. But for her own well-being, she needs to handle this situation with dignity—be kind to herself and not commit to him before he commits to her.

• Nancy prides herself on being a good mother, but motherhood has become the umbrella under which everything else is protected from the outside world. At one time Nancy was an exceptional OR nurse, and the doctors she worked with could rely on her. Her own mother worked, and she says simply and definitively, "I want to be there for my kids, give them what I didn't get. When I tell my mother how I feel, she only says, 'Guilty, guilty, guilty! I'm happy to help you but don't want to listen to you complain.'"

That she's given up her nursing career and made mother/wife a full-time job is not the issue so much as her overinvolvement with her children. Trying not to sound resentful, she told me she locks herself in the bathroom for fifteen minutes in the middle of the day to get some time for herself. "Is this my life?" she says, also fearing what her life will be like without them. Nancy is losing the "I" in her life by clinging to her children, reassuring herself that they need her by making them needy. She doesn't see the future as starting tomorrow. Rather, she takes a leap of twenty years wherein she does nothing to advance herself professionally. Thinking cynically, she dooms herself to not fitting in.

In reality, Nancy has a problem leaving the safety of home and competing in the outside world. She's a bit of a negative thinker, part of which is being a martyr and a victim, and part of which is regret. At the same time, she likes being in control and having things done her way. Her children, her home, and a generally compliant husband provide this working formula. Nancy will have to make peace with what she really wants and what it will take for her to have a life of her own.

• Finally, there's Marcie, accusing Ed of being a baby who won't grow up and pull his fair share. Her money, she insists, gives him time to write the songs no one buys, as she punctuates it, "free of annoying pressures, like paying his share of the rent." Ed charges Marcie of wielding money like a club she's always swinging at him and says it exhausts him to keep jumping out of the way. "You would rather make me feel bad about my career than see me succeed," he once accused her.

Marcie is stuck at a point where she talks about what is missing from her life and how empty she feels as a woman. And, in a way, Ed's right: Marcie doesn't really want him to succeed. She'd rather continue to lament her situation. Ed finds it painful to try to meet Marcie's criteria, and he's unable to duplicate her dynamism. What Marcie can't stand is that Ed is who he is and that she *can't* really change him or move him.

Even though she believes she has a strong ego, and certainly she is enjoying lots of financial rewards, Marcie has an "I" that is addicted to *not having*. When she realizes that what she wants is *wanting*, not *getting*, she can begin to end her suffering. She also needs to open a conversation in which she offers Ed the chance to satisfy her and not always find him wrong. The fact that Ed makes less money than Marcie is not unusual in America today. Some women resent such a situation; others do not. For Marcie and Ed, reconciliation would mean that each of them would have to accept what the other is bringing to the relationship.

Who Do You Think You Are?

Nancy once asked me one of those philosophical questions that stopped me a moment before I could answer. She said, "I know what

I like, who I love, and what really, really bothers me. But how do I know *who I am* as definitely as what I like and don't like?"

My response was, *"Who you are is who you think you are."*

She replied, "I wish that answered my question!"

What I want to make clear to Nancy is what I hope to help you with here: to know in your heart that you are the subject of your life and the object of your strength. Only you can know you and find you. It's a worthy pursuit to maturity, wisdom, and a *realized* self—your unique "I." When you get to that realized self, you feel awe, resilience, courage, and self-respect. You can manage anger and frustration. You're in touch with any false front you've put up, and can knock it down. Your realized self is capable of introspection, of giving up denial, and of respecting its intentions.

When you've defined that "I," your self is stripped of the excuses for poor behavior that keep getting you in the same kind of trouble year after year. When you have a strong "I," you understand that emotional reactivity, that is, knee-jerk responses to what others say or do, ultimately does not get you what you need in life. Your realized self will strive to make decisions based on *dignity, integrity, open-mindedness, and spirituality,* not on last resorts, designer labels, competitiveness, greed, or begrudging others.

When you've connected with the "I" in your life, it means, for example:

- Not asking others to do for you what you refuse to do for yourself.
- Figuring out who you are now and accepting that it may not be who you *were* or who *you'll be* in the future.
- Feeling connected to the larger world or a spiritual being.
- Striving to continue your personal growth.
- Making the basis of marriage a loving friendship instead of hot sex.

- Allowing your children to grow up and become adults in your eyes.
- Being able to think of something you did that makes you throw your head back and roar with laughter—experiencing joy. Or laughing at things that once seemed so serious.
- Looking at the hurt under the anger, the neediness under the ego, and being able to identify your basic insecurities and how they drive your actions.

When you have an "I" in your life, you experience real life with a *realized* self.

Most of all, your realized self—that "I" you keep refining and defining over a lifetime—is the composite of natural potential to do good and be your best. Sure, it takes work and effort, *but self-worth is impossible without self-work.* Your world changes by changing yourself, not by changing the others around you.

RETURNING TO YOUR REAL SELF: A TRUE STORY

Betty had little faith in her ability to change when she walked into my office that Saturday morning, seeking therapy more to please her sister than to help herself. She was thirty-five years old, informally dressed in slacks and a sweater, and red-eyed from a night of bourbon and mentholated cigarettes. While she struggled to talk about her life with a practiced bravado, tears ran down her cheeks. At the end of the hour, I knew I was talking to a desperately lost woman who wanted "to find herself" before her greatest fear came true—*giving up on herself.*

Betty's problem was that she lived a kind of double existence that put gambling with her life on a grand scale. Variations of her story are everywhere in America for women at every stage of life. A college graduate and divorced mother of five-year-old twins by day, Betty held a responsible job managing one of a chain of retail shops. By night, her energy, passion, and money went for drink, chasing men for sex, and, going one step further, drugs.

Because of her dissolute habits, she'd lost custody of her sons to their father. Rather than sobering her up, the loss drove her deeper into substance abuse and, she says, "a real taste for the highs of trouble." She was arrested for drug dealing after making her first and only delivery—stopped by the police for speeding and weaving on the road. A lot of cash was scattered across her lap. She spent a year in a therapeutic community, entrusting her sons to her now ex-husband and his new wife. When she got out of rehab, she went back to work for her father, but she was still unable to control her drinking.

"You can get to a point when you need too much of everything to feel good—sex, food, alcohol, drugs, and guys who like trouble more than you," Betty told me, expressing what had become her ruling philosophy. "I loved getting high, but hated being a drunk and a junkie. I did everything—got into sexual scenes, got robbed, put myself in dangerous situations with bad people, but I always managed to get to the shop and put in a productive workday, even if I felt like a zombie. The hardest thing of all is trying to pass for normal while you're out of control. You've got to keep your job, raise your kids, pay your bills, and keep your secrets. It ain't easy!"

Betty paid for her addiction to excess by more than getting arrested—she felt disgraced and worthless. Yet, she blamed everyone else around her for what she'd gotten herself into. She said that it was always the angry interactions with her father that drove her to excess and always the leaden disappointment in her mother's voice that made her feel guilty and inadequate as a woman. Betty's parents seemed to bring out the worst in her. "I humiliated myself so much, that when I looked in the mirror, I couldn't see my own reflection. *I didn't know who I was.* I was a blur, literally."

When her father became ill and retired, she took over the business. The responsibility of managing four shops at the age of thirty-two helped boost her ego. She got clean for two years, but then she started drinking heavily again when the business lost a lot of money and two shops had to shut down. Once again, Betty felt adrift in two worlds.

With her father ill and helpless, and the business crashing around her, Betty sought solace with her first substance of choice, alcohol.

The difficult relationship with her father, an alcoholic and a seductive charmer, got worse. Now Betty felt responsible for causing him more pain (on top of his illness) by nearly losing the business he'd built. Her drinking didn't change the numbers on the ledger sheets, but she deluded herself into thinking that her father "would understand why I hit the bottle." She was drinking for both of them.

Her life continued on a downward spiral. She broke up with a man she loved but who wouldn't live with her drinking. "I played the game with Mark, pushing him, making promises, and hiding the vodka," Betty told me. "I'd hide the vodka, but you can be sure I'd let him catch me loaded. Then I'd cry. He'd yell. All that. I made more promises. He knew I was full of it." The breakup, the failing business, and the haunting loss of the twins' custody all conspired to push her to the edge. Betty got drunk at a bar and while driving home barely conscious at the wheel, rammed through a plate-glass window at a gas station. The court remanded her to a treatment center for outpatient therapy.

When Betty went through that window, the sound of the glass breaking around her was both deafening and celestial. "The impact of the crash and the tinkling of the glass falling on my car kept echoing in my head," Betty said. "I realized *as never before* that I needed help and how scared I was to get it. I'd look in the mirror and say, 'Oh, God, help me,' even though I believed God had forsaken me and help would never come. When I sat there drunk at that gas station, I saw the blackness at the end of the road and knew that if I didn't get straight, I'd fall into it, go to jail, or die."

This realization brought her to my office. Betty knew that she'd been given another chance to face reality and allow herself to live. She needed to examine the problems with her family, her ex-husband, Mark, her sons, and how she'd treated them and herself—and the place of her addictions in the scheme of things.

Over the last year, she's learned to grow up and put an end to her self-destructive rebellion. She can identify and protect herself from bad influences by understanding what situations make her want to drink, take drugs, or sleep around. Wisely, she's begun to build a strong support system of people who expect better of her. She said, "I now realize that when I exposed myself to the truth about myself, good things came out of it." With growth, she has one regret about her indulgent past—that of damaging the relationship with her sons, which she hopes to repair.

"I learned something I thought I'd never say. You have to feel your pain," she said at one session with me. "I used to feel that if I allowed myself to feel pain, I would die. I believed that if I told others how I felt, I'd be punished. I believed that if I told others how I felt, they'd leave me or humiliate me. The only way out of something, even addictions, is to walk through them.

"Now I no longer care if everyone likes me or if every man wants me. Breaking promises to yourself and other people and screwing up is nothing to brag about. You don't fool anyone, especially yourself. It feels nice being healthy, and it's freeing not having secrets, even from myself. I just know that whatever happens now, I'll be okay."

Betty lived and breathed in extremes. The truth is that *controlling* excess actually requires less energy than does living in it. When excess rules, you require an enormous amount of physical and mental energy to feed and maintain the drive. Whether excess is about overeating, not eating, gambling—or, as in Betty's case, alcohol, drugs, and sex—body and mind demand satisfaction to quiet a hunger that's really coming from a spiritual source: the inner "I." That hunger, like drinking or binge eating, is always symptomatic of another longing, a longing for love, for valuing oneself, for feeling worthy. When you live in excess, you can't be serene, fully engaged in any other thought or act, nor give to anyone else with generosity.

By "wising up," Betty was able to stop victimizing herself or others for having made mistakes. It took courage for Betty to face how she lost the "I" in her life and to change the situation.

Betty's is a profound example of proving that your past need not become your future. There's power in this idea, and belief in it can bring about amazing results. As philosopher Ernest Holmes said, "Never look at that which you do not wish to experience." One debilitating belief that can create sadness and frustration is that you've reached the end and cannot change. So if you continue looking at the past, then there's no way to have a different future. A second act of self-sabotage is to reject yourself for the problems you have. If you never limit your view of life by any past experience, you can only go forward. The past is who you *were*, not necessarily who you are now or are going to be.

Most of our troubles and disappointments stem from a devaluation of our worth and the inability to forgive ourselves. We make messes or mistakes and repeat them automatically, and soon the messes are folded into a way of life. Anger, jealousy, feeling betrayed, defeatist ideas, superstitious fatalism, morbid fears of not conforming to others' demands or expectations also add to the belief that we aren't worthy of living or of love.

When you make a mistake, there's going to be a consequence. *Ignorance* about why you keep making the same mistakes is a failing, but there's actually a benefit to ignorance: it can be corrected by knowledge. If you know yourself, you're less likely to beat yourself up for your mistakes. Instead, you can face them, apologize for them, and, most important, learn from them and go on. If you believe your problems are fixed, inscrutable, and unchangeable, you wind up punishing yourself for them and never changing.

FINDING YOUR IDENTITY WITHIN AND WITHOUT SOCIAL PRESSURES

I read once that it's been said that God created humans *upright* and they became *bent* on their own. The Kabbalah, an ancient mystical interpretation of the Jewish Scriptures, says we're broken vessels, and the world is broken, too, but that it's our mission in life to recreate paradise on earth. How *do* we create paradise from so much fragmentation? It's possible *to mend our world only by finding the courage to mend ourselves.*

Of course, the forces that help shape the complex network of bends and breaks that make us unique are not entirely of our own choosing. Other, more earthbound "sculptors" have pushed here and pulled there to leave their fingerprints on us. Parental influences, peer pressure, personal talents and abilities, fulfilled and unfulfilled aspirations, passions, social change, trends, and threats to our well-being all reshape the innocence with which we started out.

Social forces shape us all. Never mind the talents and drives of young girls, there are mothers who still tell their daughters, "You can't be a painter or doctor or inventor. Be a third-grade teacher instead . . . and get married." It was once the way of the world. My own mother hoped I'd marry the butcher's son, who flirted with me when I was fifteen, so I'd always have lamb chops on the table. At the time, I thought she'd lowered the bar in terms of standards for me, but now I understand that she just wanted to be sure I'd never go hungry. It was what she knew. Following thousands of years of tradition that preceded her, she couldn't consider the idea of women having a job for any other reason than to help a husband through school.

The bend in the road changed for women with the arrival of the women's movement. But nature remains the same. Girls tend to give up some of their real selves as they enter adolescence. Girls who are intellectually gifted, or good athletes, or who want to enter the arts or be inventors, suddenly may feel ashamed of their abilities and interests. At this emotional and hormonally charged juncture, they're taught to defer to males, told what to give up to make them popular with boys—and how to wind up married to the most successful of them.

Boys, on the other hand, are raised to compete, challenge, and succeed—and along the way, toughen up and hide or deny their feelings. At an early age, they're told it's money and a higher-level career that attracts women, not who they are inside. And, sadly, many women contribute to their dehumanization. What they're looking for is what men can give them, not who they are. Is it any wonder that so many women make poor selections for husbands and fathers of their children?

Social and political change in the last few decades have given women opportunities outside the home and made working more acceptable, but emotional and spiritual change have not quite caught up. Women are still dealing with the same problems in relationships of every nature—compounded by issues of achievement not based on managing a home. So Nancy, encouraged by her working mother to find a vocation, felt that being a nurse gave her social validation, but not soul. Her inner drive took her home, to being a full-time mother. There are women who may have done less for themselves, and never tried working at what would most please them. Yet other women may be stuck in unsatisfying marriages, humiliated into subjugation or pressured to be what they're not.

So where are we? Now we've moved, for example, from a 1950s

mentality of conformity and no sex until marriage to the "right of self-expression," or anything goes, to sex on the first date and a sense of spiritual emptiness. When women learned how to say yes, too many forgot how to say no. There's no wisdom or inner fulfillment in reducing yourself to the lowest common denominator. Amy's a good example of how this can happen.

Most of all, although women have freedom as never before, many have lost their "I" and are still rebelling. *Who do you think you are?* remains the question. Who you think you are will design the rest of your life. Sometimes you can get thwarted and go down a twisting path and then come back to yourself. There are very few decisions you make that can't endure an adjustment or change. It's just that it has to be a conscious change, not acted on out of *rebellion*.

Although it carries with it a sense of energy running on all jets, rebellion is really a sputtering phase of youth, not a way of life. Rebellion when you're young helps you define your identity. In submission, you do what people tell you to, whereas in rebellion, you do exactly the opposite. Rebellion is about trying on roles, taking dares, and seeing what you're made of as you try to assert your independence. If you're twenty-five or thirty-five or sixty-five and still rebelling, you've really stayed as you were but call your rebellion something else—for example, "personal expression." Ongoing rebellion isn't a sign of having heightened your identity as an adult, but rather a nod to another form of adolescence. Going from being a scared kid to a scared woman who goes with trends for the hell of it (like getting facial tatoos or excessive body piercing) or creates chaos for herself and others shows a lack of personal growth.

Usually, rebellion exhausts itself. Many times the pendulum swings from one side to the other until it balances in the middle. When that happens, you can put emotional reactive impulses aside (like putting yourself in situations where you can get hurt or catch a deadly disease) and make a meaningful decision about who you are and how you fit into your world. (This is such an important subject that I've devoted Chapter 2 to it.)

In any society there's a difference between impulses and decision. A reactive response is experiential and sensual, not intellectual. It hinges on primitive drives and, if your life is threatened, survival. So a friend dares you to try heroin just once. If you agree, you haven't made a decision in your best interest. Decision making requires careful thought that weighs the pros and cons of an idea and can approximate the consequences. An impulse is too fast a response for real cognition. An impulse would say, "Sure, why not? I'll take a drug, and my friends will think I'm cool and making waves." A reasoned thought would say, "Thank you, not a good idea. I don't want to go to that kind of party."

In every case, the realized self can ask the question, "Do I feel I'm doing the job I want to be doing and living the life I want to be living?" and be able to answer yes.

In Sam Keene's book, *Fire in the Belly,* he tells a story of sitting at a bar after he'd just lost a love. The man at the next seat said something like, "Tell me about yourself." In talking to the man, Keene said, he realized that men have two questions they're expected to answer: "Who am I?," and "Where am I going?" Reading this, it struck me that there's only *one* question that historically women ask themselves: "Who am I going to marry?" But three questions every woman should ask herself instead are, "Who am I, where am I going, and whom do I want to take with me," in that order.

This is where it all starts and where it all leads. If you know *who you are* and *where you're going,* then you can answer any question about that "I."

"There's always one moment in childhood when the door opens and lets the future in," wrote novelist Graham Greene in his book, *The Power and the Glory.* For some of us, the door doesn't open until later in life. You've got to be ready to go through it! That opening door is a metaphor for a moment of enlightenment that tells you

you've got the power to make changes. You're in touch with the possibility of repairing the past and changing the direction of your life. You find your moment. Putting it in its simplest terms, *walking through that door is both a turning point and the act of turning yourself around.*

I know it can happen. For some women, there's an event that hits like a lightning bolt, like Betty going through the windshield and shop window. She knew she would have to stop rebelling—drinking and living recklessly—or die. It could be a daily routine taking its toll, like Marcie escaping from her children to her bathroom to reaffirm her sense of self as an adult. Or it could be something entirely different for you. Maybe it is about the stress of work getting you angry or depressed so that at night you dull the pain with prescription drugs or sugary junk food. Maybe the moment comes at an ego-deflating point in the search for a job, a separation in a long-term relationship, and even envying a friend's sudden success.

Whatever it is, the *moment* tells you that you've let your life roll by and you must act now. When that trigger goes off and the smoke clears, you can see your world for what it is. You can start by identifying what's wrong with your life. You've traveled down the wrong road, followed the wrong leader, or wrapped yourself in false fronts. In any case, life is no longer giving you any satisfaction.

There are all forms and levels of seeking that "I," your realized self. You can make an extreme change or take a series of much smaller turns, always moving toward your goal. It begins with three key decisions:

- Facing your past and understanding where you got lost.
- Being willing to adopt a better way to live.
- Giving up the belief that others must change, not you—the greatest obstacle to changing.

You can't go back and undo the past, and you can't change the world out of which you came. But you *can* give yourself the gift of finding the best "I" in your life right now. Feel who you are; don't just intellectualize. When you know in your heart that history needn't repeat itself any longer, you will go from seeing yourself as luckless to someone who makes her own luck. You will know you're not helpless, but that you can turn your life around by doing what's right for you.

It has happened to me. I was seven and a half years into hosting my CNN talk show when one morning I picked up the *New York Post* to learn that my show, *Sonya Live,* was, as the paper proclaimed, *"dead"!* It was a brutal shock, since I had not yet been told that my contract wouldn't be renewed for another season. I learned it the hard way, by reading it in print.

This is the kind of unexpected and ego-battering event that millions of Americans have experienced: the loss of a long-term job you've come to depend on. In my case, the job had my name on it, and I'd be out of work in a few months. I felt I had lost a really important piece of my *identity.*

Being a trained psychologist who put reason before emotion didn't lessen the blow to my self-esteem. On the last day of my show, I felt cast out in an offhanded way. I spent considerable time forming a brief but sincere good-bye speech to my audience. Shortly before air time, a CNN VP called me in the makeup room to tell me I would not be going on. Instead, they were going live to Bernard Shaw, then the news anchor in Cuba, and I was history.

The bureau chief then asked me to stay for a farewell party for me later that day. If I knew anything, it was that I did not want to participate in a charade, and I said so. He insisted I stay. "The party's for you," he said, "one of the CNN execs is even flying up from Atlanta to see you."

That "farewell" party, I knew, was for the morale of the staff, not really for me. I was already a "ghost" who reminded people that the same could happen to them. I told the producer, "Before I got that call telling me I wouldn't go on this morning, I had an obligation to CNN and the New York chief. Now I no longer work for you, and I don't have to do anything CNN requests of me." Then I moved up my plane reservation and wished a few colleagues good luck on my way out and headed home to Detroit.

Not showing up at my own party was politically incorrect, but, truth to tell, it gave me a great feeling of control over my life. When I walked out of the studio that Friday morning, I felt as I had when my father died: his death freed me from feeling like a rejected and unloved child. This loss freed me, too. I was hurt, of course, already missing the work and the perks of what I thought was the greatest job in America and uncertain of what to do next, but I knew in my heart that it was time to move on. CNN had made the break that needed to be made so that I could move forward.

At home, I had time to think about this thing called "career"— where it had taken me, how it had changed my life, and what its effects were on my family. For example, my home was in suburban Detroit, but I did my own show first out of Los Angeles, then New York, flying home on weekends. My husband got used to seeing the back of me rushing out the door in the middle of Sunday dinner to make a flight. I always left three days' worth of dinners in the freezer for him. I'm sure you recognize that as caring *and* guilt! I knew the airports intimately. My daughter's wedding was arranged mostly by phone. She had the good grace to give birth to her first child on a weekend, when I was home. After almost eight years of traveling back and forth across the country, I'd now have to become reacquainted with the self whose life did not revolve around a television show. I would have to re-form my family life.

The host of *Sonya Live* had car services at her disposal, no waiting in line for seats or tickets, access to many of the famous by virtue of working at CNN and some celebrity. Ticking off the perks of a glamorous job you'll probably never have again is no way to separate from it, but one morning I found I could finally let it all go. I knew that everything has benefits *and* liabilities, including a plum job. When you are in a high-pressure, highly visible job, you are called upon to make choices on behalf of company policies that you disagree with or dislike. There were also the times I had pushed for what I wanted out of my own ambitious needs at my family's expense. I had to examine these issues, too. I reconnected to my real self.

I'd been given a gift in the form of a great day job. I paid tribute to all the friends I'd made because of it and sent cards or presents. For others, I flew back to New York and hosted dinners honoring what they had given me by opening their homes and lives to me over the years.

What was important to me now? When I began to separate Sonya Friedman the woman from Sonya the host at CNN, I could see that show as a phase of my life, not my life itself. I knew the truth: everything is temporary—whether it is work or relationships. We don't own the space we occupy; we simply lease it and typically don't know when the lease will run out. It is up to us to be our best at the time, and as James Ramey, author of *Intimate Friendships*, once said, "The only thing you owe people is to leave them at least as well off as when you found them." *True*

When, like me, you fear you've lost a measure of identity, you will also accept that every life has its turning points and will realize you can get that identity back. The experience with CNN gave me the appreciation of knowing we are not our jobs, our habits, what others need from us, or a prominent body part. Once I came to grips with the real meaning of work in my life, I could begin my quest for resolution, healing, and inner peace, and I could focus on the path I would take next. All during those years at CNN, while living in both Los Angeles and New York, I kept my ties to Detroit to maintain my stability. How grateful I felt to have somewhere to go, back to people who cared about me and a profession—psychologist—waiting for the restart button.

REFINING YOUR IDENTITY: DEFINE YOUR STANDARDS AND WHAT YOU WANT

When I hear a woman say something callow like, "Why not have sex when I want? Everyone's doing it," or "Why shouldn't I get in someone's face before she gets in mine!" I know I'm listening to a woman who has dropped her standards and has an identity based on pleasing or challenging others, not herself.

Part of what I want to stress here is that you can make your life work if you keep reviewing it with as much honesty as possible while keeping your standards high. Never edit yourself out. If you have a thought that seems to shock or frighten you, write it down and weigh it. Keep revising your goals and plans until you reach the "I" that makes sense to you and brings you satisfaction.

You'll need to change certain ingredients until your identity is clear to you and your life comes out the way you want it. Eventually, you'll end up knowing who you are, what you stand for, where you're going, and what things give you joy and sense of passion, commitment, and attachment. Then, after all the work on yourself, you can ask, "Whom do I want to take with me?" as opposed to, "Who will take me along with him?"

A recipe for life can be revised at any age and changed until you get it right. I spoke to a patient who at sixty-eight years old confesses that she wishes she'd tried acting, what she wanted to do at eighteen, twenty-eight, thirty-eight, and forty-eight. But I promise you that if she stays the same and lives to eighty-eight, she'll be saying, "I wish I had taken acting lessons twenty years ago." It's hard for some people to put one foot in front of the other to begin to make a difference. Make the effort, and take tiny steps at a time.

To find the "I" in your life, come of age while reading these pages, and write your history. What had you hoped life would be like? What is it like for you now? When did you realize you were on a path you didn't expect to walk down? Do you rationalize and give yourself excuses for being there, although it makes you unhappy? Rationalizations are what you tell yourself in an attempt to divorce yourself from what's going on.

Maybe, like Nancy, you're devoted to full-time mothering, and you feel torn about reentering the work world down the line. Nancy tells herself some of the following rationalizations, starting with, "I can't make a change now because . . ."

- It wouldn't be fair to the children. No housekeeper takes care of the kids the way I do, so I couldn't go back to school/get a job.
- The world is crazy and I don't trust strangers, so I have to wait until someone I know refers me to a good firm.
- I don't have the wardrobe or the money to buy the right clothes to go out looking for a job.
- I'm too fat to go to an interview today.
- I may not luck out again and work for reasonable bosses.

I tried to get Nancy to see the truth about her situation. She doesn't want to make a commitment to be somewhere every day. She doesn't want to bring in money because she fears her husband won't give her as much for the house and will start depending on her income. Then, if he's dependent on her income, she fears she won't have a choice about staying home. She's afraid she can't go back to the OR and compete at as high a level as when she left. She fears that her future colleagues will be younger, and probably brighter and more aggressive, than she is.

Everything Nancy tells herself about herself buries her deeper in excuses. For now, she's halfway there, saying, "I'm starting to think about what I want to do when the children are both in school."

⁓

I can offer guidance and insight, but the answer is always inside you. No one else has those answers but you. No one can define yourself but you. Here are two questions to ask yourself about how you define yourself:

- *Are you honest with yourself about why you're putting things off?*
- *Do you stand up for your beliefs, or do you compromise your standards out of expediency?*

The job of adolescence is defining an ego identity. You carve out your personality against the "rock" of tradition, your parents, your environment, and social mores. I remember a friend's grandfather telling her as she embarked on her journey to college, "If you marry a Catholic, you're dead to us," and another friend's mother saying, "Don't let college make you too liberal, like getting into interracial relationships." Both statements represented the impenetrable wall of a standard, *a rock of beliefs*. That rock, right or wrong, is a boundary line in the sand.

What are your standards? What is your "rock"? Does that rock need re-examination?

- *Do you believe that others hold your fate in their hands?*

It's important not to be arrogant and believe you are a finished product who has it all together—if only others would give you what you want—or get out of the way. All of a sudden, an event can occur that forces you to continue working on this thing called life with your own efforts. When you put yourself in someone else's hands, you put yourself in the danger of losing that support or feeling a sense of betrayal. Your expectations that they will take care of you as you wish to be taken care of is unrealistic. Most people have their own agenda and will not make you first in their lives.

I find it humbling to know we're all just human beings who can be blindsided at any time. Blindsiding means that change comes suddenly to you, usually without your input or encouragement. Your husband decides to leave you for another woman and wants custody of the children. You're being supported by your parents in high style when suddenly your father goes bankrupt, or he decides it's time for you to pay your own way.

Can you be responsible for yourself while appreciating what others bring to your life?

- *Can you give up the support system that keeps you safe and go after what you want?*

"What do you want to do?" I asked a patient who is working part-time at a Madison Avenue salon she feels halfhearted about. At twenty-six years old, Sally was unable to answer the question and began to cry. The tears were important because they represented a small breakthrough for a woman who was getting by on attitude and bravado. Sally works a flex-time job paying $20,000 a year and lives in New York, where her parents pay for her luxury apartment. So although she is living in her own apartment, driving her own car, and working, that surface description of her life belies the truth: she's being infantilized by misguided and overindulgent parents. She fears that she hasn't the skills to be fully independent.

When people say, "I don't know what I like," or cry about the sense of failure connected to it, they probably haven't tried anything. Sally's passions are few. She likes archaeology, and she buys books on the subject, but she can't see it as a career. She likes medicine, but she fears she couldn't get through medical school or nursing school. She likes shopping, but this is a pointless activity unless she wants to go into retailing, open a shop, or become a designer—none of these choices interest her.

What stops Sally is that she's got a cushion: her father's money. It has helped her to the point of stagnation. She's lost passion and motivation for accomplishing anything because she doesn't have to earn a living or worry about survival. Although she's unhappy about it, she's unwilling to give anything up of the status quo to make a change. Why?

Sally's greatest fear is proving to her parents what she believes they already know about her—that she can't make it without them. And so she does nothing, too fearful to prove them right and too fearful to prove them wrong. You may understand how she feels when I put it this way: Assume that you've probably fallen on your face a hundred times. The next time you fall on your face, you get up on your feet. You may not like it, but you've been there before and generally know what will happen. Now assume that you've *never* fallen on your face. Then your greatest fear would be falling.

To claim her identity as an independent woman capable of managing her own life, Sally's first big change would be to get a full-time job and start tearing up her father's checks. She doesn't have to love the job, just keep it and learn something to take to a better job, gain personal experience, and grow into her own identity. She has to put one foot in front of the other.

Some more questions for you:

- *What are the things you hear yourself saying about your life?*
- *What gets you into trouble?*
- *Who do you blame when it happens?*
- *What do you blame others for?*
- *What are the destructive actions you have been repeating?*
- *When did your life really start going wrong?*

I want to tell you two stories that, in different ways, cover those five questions. How many times have you heard yourself say, "How did that happen to me? When did . . . [you fill in the blank] . . . start happening?" How did you miss seeing a change that you did not want encroaching on you? How did it affect your identity?

A patient told me that she's fifty pounds overweight and she didn't really pay much attention to her weight until now. What did she tell herself to not notice the difference in her waistline at five pounds over, or fifteen or twenty-five pounds over before she said, "I'm out of control and getting fat!" When did she really start letting herself go so that she could let herself gain all those extra pounds?

"I don't think of myself as overweight," Terry said. "I was always a size eight and bounced back after the kids were born. Marriage did it to me. The last two years have been a nightmare of fights with my husband. I eat all the time and don't care and don't think about it." Then Terry got an invitation to a twenty-year high school reunion and went to her closet to see what would be right for the weather. The state of her body and what she'd done to herself hit her hard. It is totally impossible to ignore a huge physical change, but you can deny what it means to you.

You don't need an invitation, a shock, or a catastrophe to jolt you into consciousness. Face and evaluate a troublesome aspect of your life, know you need help, and plan for the situation to change. If you've turned a corner and have no idea where you are, redraw the map that will take you to where you want to go.

And then there's Linda, who has just divorced a steady, good-hearted man whom she thinks of as weak. She was married to him for nearly ten years, and left him at age thirty-three because she wanted a "healthy relationship with a stronger man." Now she's thirty-five and in love with Frank, an unreliable womanizer and alcoholic who has gotten her pregnant. Meanwhile, her ex still loves her, and she relies on him as a good and trusted friend. She's still dazzled by her lover, whom she cannot control, and bored by her ex-husband, whom she feels she can push around.

Linda's father was also a womanizer and alcoholic who was in and out of her life. Seeking the love of an unavailable man is a deeply ingrained pattern. So while all the warning signs said, *Avoid Frank*, she chose not to recognize them. "You can tell me I chose not to recognize his problems because I want the relationship to work," she said, "but I know he'll be okay if I give him a chance."

It was important for Linda to tell me she was being kind and loving about Frank's not wanting the baby, or the fights they've had about support and how the baby would be raised. Linda keeps denying the truth: Frank is unreliable, and neither her condition or the arrival of the baby will change him without his own decision to change. She would tell me a disturbing story about him, then backtrack and defend him, saying, for example, "He didn't mean what he said," or, "He promises to stop drinking." She'd set up standards for him, and if he couldn't meet them, she would leave him. But not for long. She'd too soon get very needy and go back to him.

Sally and Linda deny what's happening as it is happening, hoping for a different outcome. This hoping cheats the "I" in your life.

Let's consider some more questions to help you define yourself:

• *Are you aware of your strengths and your limitations?*
Awareness of your strengths and limitations provides a meaningful, fundamental basis for the decisions you make. When you're clear about your strengths, you can make peace with your limitations, monitor them, and improve your life.

When you act according to your abilities, then you'll know when to lead, when to follow, when to get help, when to give help, when to stop lying to yourself, and when to say, "This job/this way of life/these dreams really have nothing to do with/everything to do with who I am." By gaining this kind of clarity, you can create your own destiny and reject the attempts of others to establish themselves as experts on who you are. Full awareness of your strengths and limitations requires that you also answer these questions:

• *Do you know your goodness?*

We learn a number of distinctions as we grow up, chiefly that we're "good" when we comply with others' wishes rather than our own and don't get into trouble. There's also a more practical definition of goodness that fuels the meaning of identity, integrity, and why people think they are or are not "good."

Goodness implies decency, staying in for the long run, being there to fight the fight, and reaching beyond one's own ego to forge a genuine attachment to others. Goodness is not necessarily being blindly obedient or fatuously agreeable; "not good" is not necessarily defying the thinking of the crowd, demanding change, or being a loner.

• *Do you respect your intuition?*

Intuition is not only a mysterious inner guide, it's your spiritual self calling you to attention. Intuition not only connects to silent signals in the universe, but to your sense of right and what's right for you. When you trust your intuition, a sort of third eye, you get clues that foreshadow life-changing events. Your intuition "understands" what your consciousness, busy negotiating survival, may not yet be aware of.

Many of us minimize the wisdom in intuition, allowing doubt or even fear to stop us from following up on such thoughts. "Something tells you" to end a relationship before you're hurt any more; you "feel" a friend is leading you astray about a man she, too, is interested in; you "know" you shouldn't have another child, but you also "know" that going back into the workplace won't be as tough as you hear it is. You have an obligation to listen to that inner voice and learn why it's worth paying attention to.

• *Do you live with a purpose?*

Another aspect of connecting with the "I" in your life is to *live with a purpose*. Although it's not the entire answer to the eternally asked question, "What's the meaning of life?" living with a purpose is close to it. Purpose gives your days structure, direction, and gratification. A purpose impels you to organize and use your mind, to have clarity of vision, to be aware of your needs and your dreams—and to be able to distinguish between them.

Women waste lifetimes ruminating on, but not acting on, what they wish they could do, or they hobble along behind someone else's bandwagon. When you train yourself to identify and focus on a purpose, you can accomplish what you set out to do.

A purpose may be focused on fulfilling professional goals, being a creative homemaker, expanding your knowledge or talents, engaging in volunteerism, or being the family archivist and mediator. Living with a purpose exposes a mind at work—it implies intellectual and spiritual growth and a smarter use of abilities and instincts. When you have a purpose, or mission, you awaken every morning with a sense of worth—of being here for some reason other than just existing.

FINALLY . . .

If there's any one quality that can get you through doubt, shock, grief, or change, and help you do well in life, it is *flexibility*, or *adaptability*. If you can't stand how your life is going, change it. If you don't like what a spouse or partner is dishing out, either be flexible and establish a compromise or leave so you can find someone else. But stop wasting your precious life complaining. You control the components of change: what you think, what you say, and what you do. Your life is up to you.

To what degree does life have an "I" in it for you? Here are some questions to ask yourself:

- Are you comfortably moving through life, or have you stalled?
- If you've stalled, why do you think that's so?
- Do you make choices in life, or do you let others make choices for you? Or do circumstances make the choice?
- What general guidelines or standards help you make your decisions?
- Do you use these guidelines faithfully or only when they're convenient?
- Under what circumstances wouldn't you use these guidelines?
- Is it time for you to change these guidelines?
- Do you set goals?
- Do you tend to beat yourself up or talk yourself down?
- Can you name five strengths of yours? Can you name five weaknesses?
- Write down five words that describe you, then ask three people who are close to you to do the same. Compare the lists. How many descriptive words are the same or different?
- Do you expect, hope, or demand that others will change in order to make you comfortable?
- Are you aware of what you yet need to learn?
- Do you want your life to be different? Are you willing to change, or are you not quite there yet? If not, what would it take to get yourself ready?
- Can you state what value you bring to your world, to your family, to your job, to your relationships, to your children, and to your community?
- Did you ever had a moment when you saw what you needed to do to change? Did you do it?

- Have you begun a new path? If not, why not?
- Do you hold on to bad memories so you can say, "There was nothing good about my childhood"?
- Do you prefer not to know what's going on around you? Do you feel a lot more comfortable not knowing?
- What do you give back to others?
- In the past when you behaved badly, did you excuse yourself by saying, "I was just a kid and didn't know better." When you behave badly today—and since you're no longer a kid—how do you describe your behavior now?
- What trade-offs have you made to get where you are, and what are the payoffs?
- Can you see someone else's point of view even when you don't agree with that person?

～2～

GROWING UP

*Don't Let Your Past Become
Your Future*

I was having Sunday brunch with a few old friends when a woman who once worked with my friend Janet spotted her at our table. To be polite, Janet asked Anne to join us for coffee and casually asked, "How are things going?"

This seemingly innocent question opened a floodgate of answers about what was not "going" for her: meeting good men when you're over thirty-five, getting older and having children, getting older and your life not changing, getting older and people disappointing you, getting older and watching your life fly by, getting older and seeing the end—and fearing it won't be a pretty sight!

An attractive woman, Anne was thirty-nine years old and dressed like a Britney Spears backup singer. It's a cute look, but if you're a woman nearing forty in great emotional pain because you don't have a stable love relationship and the children you yearn for, don't make miniskirts, cowboy boots, and a fringed T-shirt your signature style. If Anne's look says deceptively young and trendy, while her personality shouts uncertain and confused, my bet is that the men who respond to her are uncertain and confused, too—not the reliable and established kind of man she's seeking as a partner for the future.

With all the questions Anne tossed at us at the table, one phrase kept repeating itself in my mind as I listened to her: *Grow up, girl! Where have you been in your own life for the last twenty years? What stopped you from becoming a grown-up, or at least further along in the maturation process? Why choose an adolescent fashion look that doesn't flatter you as much as make others wonder why you dress as you do? What emotional benefits do you get by not learning from experience? What do you need to know about your-self so you can change and make your life work as an adult?*

If any one truth was made clear after this brunch encounter, it was that *you can't grow up without growing older, but you sure can grow older without growing up.* Anne's not the only woman over thirty who is still holding on to girlish thinking run by girlish emotions. I would never criticize a youthful spirit that's curious, optimistic, and high-energy. Anne's situation is entirely different. In her case, the issue is about unplugging a connection to the past that keeps burn-ing her out. Growing up is not the static end in your life, which is what Anne apparently thinks, but an ongoing process of matura-tion. This maturation creates an inner scale that can weigh what is and is not good for you.

What *is* being grown-up about? Anne isn't my patient, so I don't know her full story and how she got stuck clinging to the past, phys-ically and psychologically. But her appearance and how she talks about her concerns are revealing in so many ways. When she thinks about growing *up* and growing older, she confuses the two or comes up with one blurry definition. In the confusion, she clings to the look and the mentality of adolescence, as if dressing young would give her more time to get what she wants. It's not an uncommon way of thinking, and it has as many variations as there are women who stop themselves on the verge of growing up.

WHAT'S GOOD ABOUT GROWING UP?

I recently saw a wonderful interview with Gloria Steinem on the *Today* show in reference to a profile of her in *Wise Women*, a book by Joyce Tenneson. The subject of the book is women who are sixty-five and older and who have something important to say to the rest of us about aging. Ann Curry interviewed Gloria about being an adult and Gloria said, "There is one thing that keeps receding into the middle distance, and that is adulthood. I think when I am seventy, I am going to have to finally admit that I am a grown-up. But that's what I thought about sixty when I was fifty, and I haven't for a moment admitted that I am a grown-up."

When I thought about it, I realized that I don't hear many women talking about when they grew up, will grow up, or the benefits of growing up! How interesting that Gloria Steinem, a serious and important political activist who has changed the lives of American women, still struggles with the concept of being an adult. How could that be?

It occurred to me that some women dwell on what's missing, what will or could be taken from them, or they fear what could be next. Mostly, women mistake *growing up*, a truly enriching personal experience, with becoming unattractive, less desirable, part of the over-the-hill crowd, and invisible. Curious, I asked a number of women over thirty in my practice as well as some friends the following question: "Do you feel that you're grown up, and do you like it?" Their replies were not only wonderful, but edifying:

- "Definitely grown up. What you see is what you get," said Helen, a caterer who has recently expanded her business. "I'm very proud of that. I no longer have the need to put on a false front."
- "I feel grown up because I've always been responsible, even as a very young girl," said Karen, a health care specialist. "I feel

grown up in my professional life, but stuck in my personal life. I was talking about not meeting the right guy, and my sister said in a jokey way, it's because I have no idea who I'm looking for. It shocked me. I have to think about that a lot."

- "It's a great feeling being grown up. I don't worry about how others react to me," Diane told me. An accountant and business owner, she added, "If people ask me for my opinion, they get it. Soon enough they learn not to ask, unless they want a truthful answer."

- "I love that I don't have to prove myself anymore. I know who I am," said Marcia, an ad executive at a large advertising company. "I've driven myself crazy trying to do better and better each year," she added. "Now I have a track record, and I've built the kind of experience that tells me I can trust my business instincts. But the best is that I can say no to things I don't want to do without feeling guilty or that I've let others down."

- Janis, a medical transcriptionist who works from her home office while raising three young children, said, "I think there are three hallmarks of maturity. One is being able to set oneself aside when it's appropriate. I can forget about myself and focus on someone else when the occasion calls for it. Two is being able to depend upon myself, and others being able to depend on me. And three, despite a rare lapse, I do what I say I'm going to do. When I have a struggle, like the struggle to forgive and overcome anger, I feel like I can work through it and handle it maturely."

- Audrey, a drug-abuse counselor, told me, "Yes, I'm grown up in that I know who I am and what my values are and I feel good in trying to fulfill them. But, no, I'm not grown up in how I *live*. I'm something of a messy housekeeper. I can't keep the kind of neat and organized showcase house that I admire and associate with being a 'grown-up' woman. My husband and son always complain but I just haven't gotten to that level of feeling I could ever take care of a beautiful place. Or maybe I don't want to do it their way!"

What I hear in these testimonies are women who appreciate themselves and what they've done, and who know there's still room to grow. They echo much of how I feel, too.

I love being a grown-up, but seeing myself as a finished product has no place in my life. I like the calm that comes with maturity and the confidence gained with experience. I enjoy knowing who I am and what I believe in. I've come to appreciate the power of the word no and the pleasure of saying yes as a choice instead of an obligation. What a luxury it is to grow up instead of just growing older.

Growing up is nothing if not a highly personal, individual issue, and proceeding at your own pace is fine as long as you are moving forward. Maturity can come at fifteen or sixteen for some or be delayed until thirty or older for others. But what if it's delayed even longer for you? However maturity happens, there's no mistaking it when you've arrived. A grown-up has a full set of intense emotional responses, but the intensity is matched by the smarts that guide them. Growing up makes whatever real resources you have *glow* instead of being obscured by a cloak of confusion or pain. Giving up baby rage, little-girl patterns, and adolescent ideas and ideals marks the beginning of adulthood.

What are we clinging to? Why is there an overpowering fear of being a grown-up?

A FEW WORDS ON BEING YOUNG

Open a picture album to the ripest years of your youth, when you were sixteen, eighteen, or twenty-one. You're looking good, laughing into the camera with some friends, and just having fun. Maybe it was one of those summer weeks where you got along with your mom and dad and it's the only shot of the three of you with your arms around each other. Maybe it was the summer your stomach was flat and you felt sexy, indomitable, and alive. Maybe the background in the shot is at the beach, a lake resort, a local public pool, and you've got an arm around your big love at the time.

No matter where it was or who was with you, those pictures make you feel not only nostalgic for the day the picture was taken, but for the whole block of time called youth. Feeling sentimental, you may opt to forget the pain and lack of composure that went along with those years. If nostalgia about youth is light, then reality about those years for most of us is shadow. What was it like in true focus: It was a time of feeling unsure of ourselves, feeling insecure about what we could do, and uncertain about what our limitations might be. We were afraid of new things, new people, and the great, looming future. *But we were young, and youth has the illusion of power.*

It took a lot of work to cover up our sense of inadequacy so that others wouldn't discover it. Frankly, I'm embarrassed by the acts of bravado I sometimes employed to keep myself going. (My friends tell me they did the same.) We were so unsure of ourselves, but we were cocky girls pretending we knew everything and made no mistakes—and God forbid someone would suggest we were at fault or that something could go wrong. We behaved as if each decision we made, from what we ate or wore or to whom we dated had the word "indelible" stamped on them. Everything was a statement about us, and that statement had better be right! We can laugh at it now, but back then, fragile but swaggering egos got in the way of our finding anything funny about ourselves. We took ourselves very seriously.

Unfortunately, some women (and men, too) stop growing right around this time and never make the transition to full adulthood. As a clinical psychologist, I see this with a frequency that astonishes me. Many of my adult patients are girls and boys just grown older, remaining needy and dependent or needy and controlling all their lives. They usually have a myriad of complaints they want others to solve. These un-grown-up women and men are often heard saying things like, "Life isn't fair, and I'm always being cheated," "No one understands me," "No one gives me anything . . . they just make promises," or "If it was good enough for me, it's good enough for my kids."

And, while pretending to hang on to ideals, some women are in a constant state of rebellion, *defying maturity*.

Tom Brokaw asserts in his book on the "greatest generation" that the men who fought in World War II and lived to shape America were courageous, responsible, mature, and, visionaries, too. They were the ones who parented the boomers who grew up in the most rapidly changing America in history, during which time there were changes that impacted every domain—social, sexual, medical, technological and political.

While these changes brought new opportunities, options, and the chance to experiment, so did they engender prolonged adolescence. *Growing up* later in life suddenly became acceptable. Girls never quite became women, and boys never quite became men. And, frankly, a lot of people, including some of the "greatest generation," reexperienced their adolescence, for example, by indulging in what I call episodes of "post-marital dating" (that is, having serial affairs), emulating teen style, and going for the sensation.

The miracle of growing up is that you *continue to grow* within a balanced life. There is fun and productivity, pleasure and responsibility, earned rewards and gifts, joy and sadness. There's still hope if you feel you're stuck in a self-destructive time warp. Time has taken you to this point, and you've brought both good and not so good experiences and feelings with you. What you can begin to do right now, as you read through these pages, is to be honest with yourself:

- Give yourself the chance to see your contribution to the life you've created.
- Take responsibility for the way things turned out for you, and make a plan for change.
- Let this be the day you stop feeling singled out for hard times and dissatisfaction and feeling helpless to make improvements.
- Stop feeling sorry for yourself, and cease to be a victim! This is the day to start on the path to maturity.

What can you do so that you don't let your past become your future? In two words: *grow up*.

WHAT'S ADULTHOOD ALL ABOUT?

There are a number of words that don't interest women, and *adulthood* is one of them. If you suffer a reflex revulsion to the word, it may be from an association with it that makes you think of burdensome responsibilities, overall unpleasantness, very few laughs, and too many pains. You may not be wild about the word, but there are plenty of reasons to be wild about what adulthood will do for you.

There are a few assumptions about adulthood I'd like to clear up. Growing up isn't a state you reach once and for all, like the color and texture of your hair when you hit twelve years old as differentiated from what it looked like when you were a toddler. Growing up, no matter what your vision of it may be, doesn't happen overnight, either. The biggest myth of all is that adulthood is the finish line, implying a real end to possibilities, after which comes nothingness followed by the downhill ride to nowhere.

There are many philosophical inquiries into this thing called maturity. The psychologist and theorist Erik Erickson offered the idea that in youth "you find out who you want to be and what you care to do; in young adulthood you find out whom you care to be with, and in adulthood, you learn what and whom you can take care of."

I love the term *the realized self*, with all that sense of growth in it and the process of becoming humane, to yourself and to others. The qualities inherent in maturity help produce your dreams and aspirations—whether they are for meeting the right person, ending a turbulent and painful relationship with a parent or partner, getting along with others, or fighting an illness with courage. When you're grown up, you give yourself that queen-of-the-world ability to figuratively climb mountains instead of standing there while life hurtles down on you like an avalanche.

Maturity gives you the freedom to be you. When you marshal as much of your potential as you can, you grow. And once an objective is achieved, you don't stop there, but plan toward new goals. So, to grow, you need to know your useful patterns and qualities and one by one eliminate the rest—the self-destructive, repetitive behaviors that keep you back.

Erickson also said that in maturity, you endure a series of tests and crises that really carve out your character. The results and resolutions of those tests and crises are part of how you know who you are, and they tell you that you can survive and make it. If you're immature, you may refuse to be tested in the many ways that are put to you every day. You won't apply for a job you're qualified for because it has a title you don't feel you're confident enough to fulfill. You won't trust any man in a relationship because the one guy you loved and proposed to you changed his mind. You won't try to heal a relationship with a parent because you don't want to open old wounds. In other words, you'd rather be miserable in what you know than try a different approach.

Which leads me to *a good working definition of maturity*: it is an ongoing growth process fueled by blood, sweat, and tears. With all the thought and effort, plans and feelings that go into growing up, nothing is as important as taking the following four vital indicators of maturity into your life.

1. *Taking responsibility for who you are and not looking to others to provide what you need.* Control of your life isn't possible if you dodge issues and blame (or look to) others to solve your problems. When you're responsible—that is, aware and responding to what's happening *to* you or *around* you—you handle your own life. Conflicts large and small force you to make decisions and will always reveal who you are as a woman. Do you really want to hand those choices over to someone else?

2. *Accepting that pain and disappointment are parts of life.* There's no getting away from it: there are, and will be, painful experiences in your life. While it's rarely a feeling most of us seek out, pain has its place—it is a messenger, not a curse, and one indicator that tells you you're alive. In no uncertain terms, distress communicates the location of emotional sore spots the way that physical pangs clearly signal where the body's weak points are. The mind, like the body, tells you where it needs healing. Pain tends to accompany the labors of accomplishment, the shock of change, and some of the frustration in struggle. Sometimes speaking the truth to another is painful, but it may be necessary so you can move forward. In all, a little discomfort is a small price to pay for learning to make mature choices.

3. *Living with ambivalence and ambiguity*. Most of us would prefer it if life's choices were black or white, right or wrong, easily made and had   predictable consequences. Life doesn't always work out this clearly or conveniently. Life is something else. As a result, the decisions we make may be fraught with confusion arising from ambiguity and ambivalence. There's a difference between the two: *Ambiguity* creates uncertainty. You're not sure what to do. A male friend says, "Maybe we'll go to a movie this weekend. I'll call you," leaving the plans ambiguous and you wondering whether or not you'll be going to that movie with him. *Ambivalences* involve two contradictory feelings. Taking the preceding example, assume you're angry that this man left you on hold and you feel like making other plans so he won't treat you like this again. He's being non-committal, and you don't like it. On the other hand, you really like him and don't want to be out if he calls.

Wish for it all you will, but there will never be a world of absolutes and guarantees. Actually, the only guarantee is that there is no guarantee. Dates are broken, promises are breached, contracts are disputed, and sometimes you demand an answer from someone who just doesn't have the answer *yet* and who may never have the answer. When you know there are no absolutes and your world might change suddenly at any time, you can accept the fact that *uncertainty offers possibilities and that rejection isn't a terminal disease.*

Living with ambivalence was harder to endure when you were young, wanted specifics, and saw everything in black-and-white terms. When you're an adult, you know there are infinite shades of gray, and there will be other occasions to make similar choices. While any frustration is uncomfortable, if you accept the fact that ambiguity and ambivalence exist in the course of normal life, it lessens your daily stress.

Whatever the conditions in your world, when you're mature you can *say what you mean* and *mean what you say* and make yourself clear.

4. *Knowing the distinction between being tamed by, and tested by, life.* We used to think that a mature person was tamed by life—the person who slowed down physically, gave into safe routine, and relinquished dreams. A general mind's eye image of this kind of "maturity," then, was a musty being whose only activity was flaking away. But true maturity is quite the opposite.

When you grow up, you become less timid, less restricted, and better able to make more and riskier choices. When you cling to the "side rails" for protection—with your past or your parents representing the safety of "side rails"—you can't step out into new experiences. Unless you let go, you won't know what you can and can't accomplish. Overprotection doesn't allow you to carve out your character, but instead, stifles your growth and blocks you from knowing your potential.

The preceding four principles of growing up dovetail into another set of four "rules" for living. I recently became interested in prayer beads and began a study of them. I found that the first prayer beads were of knotted strings; in fact, the fringe hanging from the undergarment of observant Jews consists of knotted strings. I asked a rabbi to explain them to me and heard something so profound, I want to share it with you.

The fringes are made so that one-third of the strings contain four knots, and the other two-thirds hang free. The rabbi explained that the four knots stand for *dignity, integrity, open-mindedness, and spirituality.* "The ancients," he said, "say that if you spend time working on those four knots and make them a part of your daily life, you can spend the rest of your time conflict-free." How simple it is to make choices when you have a foundation of ideals to reach for. How much easier it is to give up grandiosity, arrogance, insecurity, and the incompetence you experience in youth when you have some fundamental values to hang on to. What are your fundamental values? Can you see that the four listed above might make your life easier?

WHAT'S IMMATURE? TAKING STOCK OF PATTERNS WORTH DISCARDING NOW

At the simplest level, maturity is about *unlearning immaturity*. Since there's an enormous amount of self-absorption in immaturity, it can be tough to go from "I want it when I want it" to "I will do my utmost to get what I want without hurting others and when I get what I want, I will be happy with it." When you unlearn what's immature, you go from being girls to being wise women.

Let's go back a moment. Psychologists who study the behavior of young children can tell you that children believe adults understand what they're feeling without their having to verbalize it. In this way, a child tests the love, tolerance, and sensitivity of her very narrow world. But an adult doesn't have to resort to child-like games or trick questions. Yet, many women resort to this childlike testing and bury their true needs in a muddle of confusing behavior. I know you've heard what it sounds like. For example: "*You* tell *me* why I'm mad," or "Don't ask me to explain; you know what I mean," or "If you don't know why I'm upset, I'm not telling you." Such statements make no sense when you're a grown-up.

Maturity is rich with your experiences, memories, and feelings from yesterday along with goals, dreams, and feelings for the future. Maturity is the ability to go with the turn of events and recognize that you may not have control of them instead of insisting that you do. I have a patient named Franny whose boyfriend has custody of his two small children and therefore doesn't like staying over at Franny's house. John insists on getting back home by one in the morning. He knows his kids want him to come home and be there, even if they don't need him in the middle of the night, and that the baby-sitter doesn't like being at his house alone all night.

Yet, Franny's ongoing fight with John is about her demanding that he stay overnight. By telling him, "You can't go . . . you're staying over!" she's pushing him to make a choice between her and his children. Another man might give in, but John will not. He's being mature about protecting his kids. She's being immature about pressuring him to prove his "love" to her.

What else is worth giving up in immaturity? A lot. In her article on growing up in *Vogue* magazine, writer Amy Gross said that maturity is about being a pro at the life game. That is, maturity knows what you really want to keep score on and *immaturity* keeps score on everything. I've come up with a list of qualities that keep scorecards full and may be blocking your chances of growing up. Once you admit to a trait, you've taken the first brave step. Then you can begin to change. Immaturity is marked by

- Self-effacement (putting yourself down) and self-absorption.
- Being undisciplined.
- Rumor-mongering and jealousy for its own sake.
- A "victim mentality" hinging on an inability to take responsibility for your own life and blaming others.
- Excusing bad behavior and asking others to excuse yours.
- Showing rage when you're criticized or when others don't agree with you.

To move toward maturity, look at the following patterns in greater depth. See if any of them remind you of what you may need to let go of.

Impulsivity, or Jumping in Without Checking to See If There's Water in the Pool

When you're young, you've got a lot of energy and imaginative ideas of what's fun, what's risky, and what's out of perspective in your daily world. Youth loves to push past the limits. So a friend throws out an idea of doing something for the hell of it, and you throw one back at her. The range of impulsive acts can go from the ludicrous to the extreme, such as binging on a quart of superfatted ice cream, getting your bottom lip double-pierced, shooting a drug "just once," seducing a married man you're attracted to just to prove you can do it, or shoplifting at the mall.

You take the challenge, but why take the risk? Maybe you wanted to come off hip to a friend or prove to yourself that you're not afraid to push the ethical boundaries you were raised on. Often your actions are prompted by the need for immediate gratification or attention and a failure to consider the consequences.

In youth, reason fades into the shadows beside the big special-effects displays that go with "totalistic," fatalistic, sensationalistic, a-zero-or-a-ten, all-or-nothing thinking. When you're impulsive, you're much more likely not to weigh the consequences of your actions. When you're immature and impulsive, you have unrealistic expectations—that you can't lose, that you will get what you want right now, or that you won't get caught. Impulsive women may also expect their agendas to have priority in the lives of others and thus see life in extremes, wanting things to be perfect or wanting nothing at all.

Personally, I'm happy to be a grown-up because I'm no longer at the mercy of my impulses. I am rarely driven by the sheer hedonism, thrill-seeking, or emotional reactivity and function of youth. Today I usually think things out. My life is more head and less nerve endings. When you grow up, you know the difference between being spontaneous and seizing an opportunity versus taking an impulsive act that is probably not in your own best interest.

Wanting Others to Make the Choices

Perhaps you think it's nice having your loved one/spouse/friend make the reservations for the restaurant, decide on the movie, book the flight and hotel for your trip to Mexico, and even pay for it all.

You know he knows what most pleases you, so you figure, why discuss it? Maybe you wanted a ring for your birthday and gave him the name of the shop where you saw the one you want. You're sure he'll pick exactly the one you want without your telling him which it is.

One consequence of trusting that he knows what you want—and that he wants the same for you—is that he might order in pizza with the works, rent a Jackie Chan movie, and make reservations at a one-star hotel, reasoning that you're in Cancun for the beach and the sun, so a low-rent tiny room with a view into the parking lot doesn't matter. Or he might go to the shop of your choice, but buy a hideous baroque thing, something you would never wear. Maybe you feel hurt. You didn't get what you want because you didn't tell your loved one exactly what that was, so don't blame him.

Immature thinking is the culprit—in this case, a belief that others are psychic and know exactly what you want without your having to describe it. If you say, "Do this or that for me" without clarifying your needs and then complain, "I don't like the way you're doing it," you're stuck in baby talk. Moreover, when those choices made for you are not right, you feel resentful.

At a meeting of staff members for a woman's support clinic, I shared my views on women making their needs clear to their significant others. "Why do we always have to teach others how to treat us?" one counselor asked. "Why don't they learn on their own?"

Whenever I hear that question, I find it fascinating that women ask it. My answer is that *part of being a grown-up is telling someone what you want.* Think of the idea of imparting information and how it adapts to other parts of your life. When you start a new job, you ask for or receive direction and information so you will have the best chance of doing the job correctly. You could not do it any way you so choose and get approval! When you learn a new sport or game, knowing the ground rules or reading the instructions precede the doing. Did you ever know anyone who sat down to play a game of bridge for the first time without some instruction? Isn't the woman herself the best source of information about how she wants to be treated?

I'm often fascinated by the degree to which men and women differ in sexual situations. When they make love, a man has little or no trouble telling or showing a woman how he likes to be touched, but a woman is typically silent, even if she hates the way he's making love to her.

It's time women learned to behave differently.

The solution grown-up women use is to be confident and state what they want, or to go ahead and make the decisions for both. If you tell your partner what you want and he doesn't like it, you've got a point at which to debate and compromise. If your partner says, "I don't care; you choose," don't waste time pushing him to be the master of the universe. Instead, take control of the situation. This way, you get exactly what you want, there are no big surprises, and you're not disappointed. When you're in charge, you get to choose the restaurant, the movie, or the hotel, or whatever's on the calendar.

Does this take-charge tactic offend men? I suggest that what happens is a reasonable division of labor. As a couple, you're better at some things, he at others. Let him appoint you the CEO of recreational activities, while he is CEO of handyman stuff, or vice versa depending on your skills. Perhaps he's the primary breadwinner and you're in charge of dealing with parents and extended-family issues, or vice versa.

Wanting Others to Do for You What You Won't Do for Yourself

I heard a story about a New York woman named Collette and thought she was a classic example of someone whose mantra is, "Poor me." Collette is a very talented artist who works religiously at her table on weekends, turning out wonderful realistic still-life paintings and beautiful drawings of her sister, who is a dancer. During the week, Collette works for a nonprofit company, being underpaid for her computer skills and managerial duties.

Collette's friends all give her pep talks about asking for a raise, since she's still making the same salary she did five years ago. Instead of looking for a better job, she offers up as valid the same lame excuses her bosses give her: no money for a raise because . . . [you fill in the blank]. None of her friends believe she's really asked because Collette always says, "I'm no good at it." This living-by-default also keeps her from having the career she wants, which is to be a full-time artist whose work sells. For this to happen, she's got to get exposure for her work—it needs to be shown in galleries and art shows.

Collette's got her portfolio in order, but it sits on a chair by the door. She can't get herself to call the reps or galleries she needs to contact. "I'm no good at it," she says predictably. Then she asks one of her friends in sales, Penny, who has bought a few of her drawings to represent her. "I wish you'd become my agent so you can promote me." Penny turned her down, saying, "I can't because I don't know how to talk about art. You should be able to do this by now for your-self. Call a real agent and get an appointment!"

Penny had an insightful take on Collette. "I know she asked me to try to sell her work only because I've got thicker skin about the world than she does," Penny said. "I'm good at listening to people and getting turned down. If I don't make a sale, it's a setback, but it rolls off my back. I just keep at it. I think Collette is afraid to ask for what she wants because she doesn't want to hear 'no' or 'maybe.'"

Collette's seeming timidity has another dimension: it's not that she's "not good at" and "can't" promote her work, but that *she wants others to do it for her*. The question she needs to ask herself is, "why won't I do it? Why can't I at least call an artist's rep, if I can't go di-rectly to a gallery?" How much does she want to have her work out there in the world and get acknowledgment for her talent? The answer is that Collette has built her fear of rejection into something more important to her than reaching her goal. We typically use a disabling word like "can't" as a way of sparing ourselves. Meanwhile, Collette is hoping her friend will change her life, or if not, maybe destiny will be on her side and one day she'll be discovered by accident.

We hear the word no all the time. Sometimes we're the one saying it and sometimes we're the one receiving it. Rejection is not a terminal disease, and you cannot assign the task of others creating your life for you. Daniel Levinson, in *Seasons of a Woman's Life*, says that youth is about God taking care of you, but that in the final analysis, you have to take care of yourself. If maturity is freedom, so is it the best of self-reliance.

Defining Yourself as Misunderstood

A patient was telling me about her husband, a forty-year-old salesman with a severe immaturity problem. Paul is spoiled. Paul's family history, according to Rhoda, is defined by his being the golden boy, the oldest child in a family of four boys, and indulged by his parents. He never really grew up or moved away from the position of being the favored one. In effect, his parents stunted his growth. Paul has never fully recovered from the shock of living in a world that doesn't comply with his wishes simply because he's alive.

Rhoda knew he was a bit of a dreamer when they married. Their courtship also showed her that being with Paul would mean she'd have to serve his needs a lot of the time and tell him he was wonderful. She *wanted* him to be wonderful in the way that she thought husbands are wonderful, and he wanted to be seen as wonderful just because he's alive. Rhoda wanted Paul to be the adult head of the household.

Paul has brought to his fifteen-year marriage the deep-seated belief that he's entitled to gifts, favors, and to say and do whatever he wants. More to the point, he cannot face how he destroys his opportunities on the job and treats Rhoda badly in his marriage. To Rhoda, Paul is the one who's responsible for his life. To Paul, Rhoda is responsible for his failure. In his immaturity, he complains that she doesn't "understand" him in as many ways as there are hours in the day, that she's a failure as a wife of an executive on the rise, that her pressuring him to get and hold any job distracts him from thinking about where he'd best fit in, that she diminishes his efforts at being a father to their two daughters, and that he resents having the burden of making most of the money to keep them afloat.

Paul's sense of entitlement also has a dimension of all-or-nothing thinking. When you're indulged, you lose your sense of autonomy and, unfortunately, indulgence doesn't ask you to grow, grow up, or grow independent. When his parents told him he was wonderful, blessed, brilliant, and the world would deliver just because he exists, Paul bought the story. It is counterproductive to tell your children they are wonderful *only because* they are as they are. You are not asking them to stretch and grow. You are suggesting that they are already accomplished as people—but how could they be?

It's actually more constructive to tell a child, "You are unique, resourceful, talented, and you can aspire to anything, but keep your feet on the ground and own up to your limitations and whatever obligations you have to others." Being pampered keeps you tied to the past. You get older believing you're the heir to the throne, but in the grown-up world, you find out your kingdom does not exist. And while Rhoda objects to how she is blamed for Paul's disappointments, she also pampers him between fights. "Sometimes it's just easier," she rationalizes.

Words are very powerful. When someone uses catastrophizing language to describe how they feel, using you as a target, you feel the effects of those words at the gut level. In Paul's case, Rhoda hears accusations like, "If it weren't for you, I'd be at the top," or, "My life is terrible because of you," or, "No matter what I do, you are an obstacle to my getting a break." Psychologist Albert Ellis wrote about the power of language and how we operate from what we tell ourselves. So when someone blames you, and you accept that blame, you create problems for yourself.

There are other conflicts coming out of language. For example, when you tell yourself, I *need* as opposed to I *want,* or he *must* as opposed to I *would like him to,* or you *should* as opposed to *please consider this,* you get into trouble. The other person feels pressured by your making a demand instead of offering an invitation. And you continue to feel entitled to a particular response, a behavior over which you have no control.

It would be in Rhoda's interest to explore (1) why she feels entitled to Paul's behaving as she would choose to have him behave, (2) why she accepts the responsibility he throws at her, and (3) why she married him in the first place, knowing who he was.

Not Being Adaptable and Denying What's Really Going On

When I was hosting my TV show on CNN, I asked my kids and husband not to call me an hour before I went on the air unless it was an emergency. During my eight years at the network, my family honored my request, and it meant a lot to me. My reasoning was simple: they were in Detroit, and I was 1,500 miles away in L.A. I could do little about solving a personal problem involving my husband, son, or daughter that very moment or do anything about a leak in the basement or a broken doorbell. It's not that I wasn't interested in problems large and small. Rather, I had a job to do and couldn't allow myself to become absorbed with family issues I knew would distract me from paying attention to doing my job properly just before going on the air. There was no way I could think about problems at home and perform well at work.

My family was wonderful about it. They understood. Their behavior was grown-up. Not everyone is this lucky with their family or coworkers. For example one of my patients is married to a surgeon at a small local hospital and has an eight-year-old daughter whom she cannot control. Vicki told me that when Debby is being difficult, she'll call her husband Jack even if she knows he's on the way to the operating room and say in an agitated voice, "Your daughter doesn't listen to me!" This is not a good time for Jack to hear these complaints, since he cannot do anything about controlling his daughter while he's on his way to perform surgery.

I tried to strongly get across to Vicki that not only is her husband unable to make a difference at that point, but she's passing an emotional burden on to him as he's about to do a life-or-death job in which he must be focused and precise. We can all sympathize with feelings of panic or powerlessness, but she needs to stop and look at how she has created this situation. Vicki does not know who the parent is and who the child is, thus her daughter runs over her— and then Vicki attempts to run over her husband. Unless Debby is trained to respect her parents and live within boundaries of reasonable behavior, this child will never learn self-control, increasing the possibility that she will get into real trouble in her teen years.

My patient, Vicki, reaches her own emotional limits. Being so tied up in her own frustrations, she loses her perspective on what her husband is doing and what his own psychological needs might be. Vicki just charges in. She wants to share her frustration, but it could wait till he comes home. In truth, she resents that Jack is not at home and therefore doesn't have to deal with their daughter's babyish behavior the way she does. Calling him says, "You haven't escaped. I'm pulling you back in." Vicki will have to make big changes to save herself, her child's future, and her marriage. Her immaturity has led to a lack of adaptability.

When you talk about adaptability, you talk about being confrontational with yourself about reality. If you're dropped in the jungle, you need to check the bushes, listen to sounds, get rid of excess clothing, and tread lightly. You cannot deny that you're in a jungle and tell yourself the gardener quit and that accounts for the overgrown landscape. To survive, you must adapt. The same is true with personal issues or interpersonal concerns in your community.

What is *really* going on around you, and how do you set up a system of checks and balances to maintain some sort of harmony without putting others at risk? Vicki has gained thirty pounds in the last year. She wants to lose the weight and look good again, she wants her child to behave and be liked by others, and she wants to stay married to Jack. The problem is that Vicki jumps ahead to the end result in her head, but she doesn't want to do the work to get there. This is the difference between those who change and those who do not. Some people refuse to take responsibility for change and go into hysteria modes instead.

Vicki tries to jump from the mess she's made to the paradise she wants by *convincing herself that she's not causing some of the problems*. What I find interesting about Vicki is that all the qualities that she dislikes in her husband are in many ways descriptive of her. She's bullheaded, doesn't want to change, is very judgmental, and wants to run away from the truth.

In immaturity, she denies what she's doing, how she's doing it, why she's doing it, and the effects her behavior have on herself and others. She once said to me, "I know I deny things. It gets me through." But it doesn't! Everything she denies comes back to haunt her. She'd be smarter to square off with herself and make the effort to adapt, change, and make a difference.

HOW TO NOT LET THE PAST BECOME YOUR FUTURE

I have a pillow in my office that says, "If you always do what you've always done, you'll always get what you always got." The quote from the Ann Kaiser Stearns's book *Coming Back* makes people smile because they see the ironic wisdom in it. Live as you do, and you can expect life to go on as it was. Obvious? Simple? Not for most of us. Change is difficult, but it's your life, and you have this moment to make it better. You change your world when you change yourself. You'll "always get what you always got" unless you make a commitment to face your problems, be willing to change, and then put one foot in front of the other in teeny little steps.

What can *you* do so that your past does not become your future? First ask yourself what is there in your past that you don't want in your future. What personal issues of your past should you have grown out of? Of course, you might say that much of the past was wonderful, but then life changed. There was a turning point. Figure out what has made the present so difficult. Is there some incident in the past that you have not examined so that it still has a deep effect on you? Is there an event that you've denied because it makes you too embarrassed to think about it or it's too painful to bring to full consciousness? What part of your life did not turn out as you thought it would? What were the circumstances? Take a look at your life now and see where the similarities are in terms of how you feel, whom you're with, and whom you choose to allow to affect you and the choices you make.

It is in your interest to reflect on these issues and do something about them. There's no absolute form to use: just do an autobiography in any way that's most comfortable for you. Write it down on paper, tape it, work it up on your computer, or talk about it to a trusted friend. I know a woman who woke up one morning when she was thirty-seven years old remembering an incestuous sexual experience with her father that she'd blocked out for twenty-five years. Nora is a paralegal and also a serious quilter with an artistic flair. She bought a box of crayons and drew a picture, with captions, of her father's seduction of her when she was twelve years old. It took her a few weeks to complete a forty-page book of drawings that got the feelings out and helped clear up some of the "whys" in her life. She cried all the way through, but that was part of the healing.

If you are haunted by a sense that life cannot change for you, it's time to turn on the light and look at what's holding you back. There are holdovers, patterns of immaturity you need to examine.

⌒

To really clarify the differences between immature and mature behavior, here are *ten very specific measures of being a grown-up*. Read them to figure out where you are and which traits you need to work on:

1. You can make decisions and live with them.
2. You can live with ambivalence and ambiguity.
3. You realize that rejection isn't a terminal disease.
4. You cope with life's difficulties rather than running from them.
5. You've given up rescue fantasies.
6. You acknowledge your fears and have learned to climb over them.
7. You've given up perfectionism.
8. When the heat is on, you don't add to it, but step back until you cool off.
9. You don't allow others to dictate your behavior—you realize you don't have to respond.
10. You listen to criticism since it typically has a grain of truth. Instead of having a negative knee-jerk reaction, you analyze its worth.

FIRING UP THE COURAGE TO GROW

The bottom line is, *change is choice*. You can either hang on to destructive, immature patterns that don't work, or go through a short period of discomfort that heralds a better tomorrow. Despite your concerns about what may lie ahead, you can stir up the courage to affect your own life. That courage can be both a turning point and the actual act of turning yourself around.

When I talk about courage, I mean that you do not back away from or avoid what you fear, but master it. This mastery begins by knowing you feel a loss of control in the face of what scares you, *then going on*. The ultimate fear is of "not being," or death. All other fears spring from this primal fear in a variety of ways. Courage isn't about deadening your feelings so you go into emotional overdrive and act mindlessly, the way that movie superheroes do. Instead, the reality of courage is in knowing what you *believe* in, feeling it, and stepping up to it. You're growing!

Here is the process:

• Begin with an accurate definition of which people, principles, or things are worthy or unworthy of your devotion, commitment, or even fear. Once you know this, you will have the intellectual and emotional courage to follow your beliefs and principles so that you'd fight to defend your rights, your home, those you love, your beliefs, your country without any doubts. This way you can more easily see what lies ahead of you, the boundaries, the sharp peaks, the smooth trails, the change of seasons, and you can handle it. You're growing!

• Understand who and what is mean-spirited, life-draining, dangerous, or evil, so you can resist those destructive forces. This way you won't side with anyone whose beliefs are founded on diminishing you on a daily basis, or destroying you, your family, or your neighbors. When you're grown-up, you can defend what you know is right.

• Like Vicki, or any young mother or aspiring mother, you have a duty to protect anyone to whom you've pledged your care or support. Giving a child her own way but then complaining about it keeps you in a self-imposed position of "victim." When you learn how to care for others, you're there for them. You also know how to respect their feelings and needs and can spare them for the time being. On a grander scale, you need to consider what would compel you to run into a burning building to save others.

• Being grown up gives you the ability to level with others (especially if you feel they are hurting you or not doing what's best for themselves) and to hear what others have to say to you. Truth-telling may be tough, because it takes courage to stop living with hypocrisy and instead live with integrity. But it's worth the effort.

FINALLY . . .

Once you know what you believe in, action comes easier. Everything you do brings you closer to who you really are—and makes better connections with others a lot more possible! Here are some questions to ask yourself about growing up:

- Do you consider yourself a grown-up?
- What does it mean to you to be a grown-up?
- How did your life change when you decided to be a grown-up?
- What, if anything, do you fear might happen should you become a grown-up?
- What is the most grown-up decision you've ever made?
- Do you miss anything about being younger, and if so, what?
- Can you think of ways to make whatever it is you miss age-appropriate?
- Do you resist being a grown-up? Why?
- Do you find yourself repeating the past?
- Do you see signs that the past is catching up with you again in time to resist, or do you discover this problem after the fact?

- Can you confront painful events in your life?
- Do you still feel "baby rage" in which you find yourself exploding at the same trigger remarks or events? What are you still mad at?
- Are you comfortable confronting people who are abusive to you, including family members?
- Are you willing to give up impulsive responses and instead think before acting?
- Do you know what you want in life?
- Do you blame others for not getting what you want?
- Do others blame you for their situations?
- Are you willing to do the work to get what you want?
- Do you learn from experience, or do you find you're always asking yourself why you get the same results from what you do?
- What have you defended and stood your ground for, no matter how much others fought you or protested?
- What tests did you rise to that helped you get through a crisis?
- Do you cling to your version of protective "side rails," and can you let go one finger at a time?
- Do you expect others to read your mind and give you what you want, yet resent them when they say they "know you?"

3

UNDERSTANDING THE MOTHER–DAUGHTER RELATIONSHIP

Am I My Mother?

- "My mother wanted more for me than what she created for herself. She was practical, too. 'Don't plant dandelion seeds and expect roses,' she said. She died too young and didn't live to see how I turned out. I'm sure she'd be smiling," says Beverly, age thirty-three, married.
- "I always felt like a cat to my mother. She fed me and changed my litter box. Sometimes I was noticed and sometimes I was not. She took care of me to the letter of the law. She took care of the law of mothering, but not the spirit of it," says Polly, age forty, divorced, and pregnant with her first child.
- "She is a good mom, who wants me to have a good marriage and a big family. I love my mother and I worry about disappointing her," says Annie, age twenty-one, single.
- "I was the last-born girl of three, of little interest to my mother and treated like a foster child. I was very smart in school, which made her proud, and I liked cooking with her, which made her feel connected to me as long as the spoon was in the pot. She was otherwise brutal and I couldn't wait to leave that house," says Catherine, age sixty-two, divorced.

Growing up, we all yearn for the perfect mother. Affectionate, protective, encouraging, good-humored, attentive, formidable but fair, generous, and full of good advice that always works out. And if these quotes from a range of women twenty-one to sixty-two years old tell us anything, it is that the "perfect" mother may exist, but few of us have ever had the pleasure of having her for our very own. What *does* exist for nearly all of us is the flawed mother, who, like it or not, is the most powerful influence on you as you grow up to womanhood. She probably did her best for you *within her abilities to be a mother,* no matter how lacking you feel she was.

The experience of being mothered may be different for each of us, but what all women have in common is a profound and multi-layered psychological bond to our mothers. However positive or negative it was, is, or turns out to be, you'll carry the mother–daughter relationship with you throughout life. You may love and cherish your mother, or you may feel little but anger toward her. Maybe you see yourself in her, or make it a goal to be as unlike her as possible. Maybe you adore her and seek out her company, or see her only to meet an obligation. Wherever you are in life, your mother's there with you in some way.

The first person to "tell it like it is" was your mother. She was the first person to tell you what the world is like from a woman's point of view and what you needed to make a fulfilling life. Along the way, she also created conflicts, fears, and crises of confidence. Almost no other relationship is as intense and emotionally loaded as the mother–daughter dyad.

It is the intensity of the relationship that made me wonder if there's been any significant shift in how mothers and daughters relate to each other now. Thus, I created my "Mother–Daughter Questionnaire." The answers to my questions brought up so many fundamental mother–daughter issues, it would take volumes to explore them all. Instead, I'll focus on a few of the most important themes that came up again and again among the forty-two women who participated in the survey.

THE MOTHER–DAUGHTER QUESTIONNAIRE

Many years ago, I worked with a group of ten women, and after a night of hearing "mother stories," I asked how many of them loved their mothers. Nine women raised their hands. Then I asked how many *liked* their mothers, and one woman raised her hand. That struck me as noteworthy.

In our society we tend to take the meaning of *like* and remove it from the meaning of love. The disconnection between the two begins early on in life, with the primary mother–daughter relationship, and the discrepancy carries over into choosing a mate. This could be one reason why women can make such bad choices in the men they marry: they believe that intense feeling and the passion it inspires can continue to exist without enjoying the man's company, appreciating his qualities, and valuing his values—that is, *liking* him. A healthy love creates a bond that is intensified by liking someone.

Over the years in my practice, I've heard thousands of mother stories, both glorious and terrible. Women of all ages have become accustomed to talking more openly about how they feel. I decided to go deeper into the investigation of the "love/like" discrepancy, and wondered if the nature of the psychological bond between mother and daughter had changed over the last thirty years. I was interested in how feminism did or didn't influence the kind of messages mothers give daughters. What have women who are now in their twenties learned from their mothers, and, at the other end of the spectrum, how does that compare with what women who are sixty-plus years old have been told? How does the relationship with their mothers affect how they choose mates?

In my generation, parents pretty much ruled, and girls were expected to be like their mothers or do as their mother asked, usually following advice like, "Get married out of high school," or, "Go to college, get a job, then get married." Most did; some didn't.

The forty-two women I surveyed were between the ages of eighteen and eighty-three, living in communities that spanned the inner city to upscale exurbia. They were never-married women, single mothers, divorcées, one widow, and married women with and without children. These are the twelve questions I asked them. Please answer them for yourself:

- What did your mother want for you? What did she want you to be like?
- What was her message to you about being a woman?
- Did you share her dream of what she wanted for you?
- What did you want for yourself?
- Have you achieved it?
- Does your mother appreciate and accept who you are and how you live?
- What message would you give your daughter if you (have) had one? Would it be different from the one you received?
- Was your mother a good mother? If so, how? If not, why not?
- In either case, is there something she could have done better as a parent?
- Are you a good daughter? If so, how? If not, why not?
- In either case, what could you do better as a daughter?
- Is there still a "hot-button" issue between you and your mother that always precipitates a fight or bad feelings? What is it? Why do you think the problem has not been resolved?

The results of the survey gave me some insight into how women think intergenerationally and reveal a fairly accurate picture of what women feel about their mothers, and about *being* a mother.

The mothers of women who are now in their fifties and sixties were given very specific life messages. These older mothers, now in their seventies and eighties were generally advised by their own mothers, "Be happy, have a family and children, learn how to cook, and have a skill to fall back on." These are messages about following tradition, looking to your mother as a general role model, fitting into society, and being practical. Husbands may leave by death, divorce, or desertion, so you need to be able to take care of yourself and your children. The messages were very clear.

The daughters of those women, now in midlife, were the generation that made the women's movement possible. They are giving their daughters similar messages, but not in the same order nor in the same language. The messages that came up in my survey consisted of three points of view: (1) get an education, be independent and successful, and consider getting married but know yourself first; (2) put marriage and family as your first goal; and (3) recapitulate my life, or, become what I want you to be, not what you want for yourself. These were mothers who could not accept that their daughters would grow up and away from them. And there were mothers who had ambitions they wanted their daughters to fulfill for them. The third category included the greatest number of mothers, those who did not show any sensitivity to their daughters, and pointed out what was wrong rather than what was right with them.

Was she a good mom or a bad mom? I found the following:

- Twenty-eight women said they had good mothers, many adding that "she did the best she could." What qualities made mom good? They said it was unconditional love, being a good role model, sacrificing, caring, loving, and being open-minded, adventurous, and warm.

- Thirteen women said their mom was not a good mom. What made mom a bad mom? She wasn't loving or lovable, didn't show affection, didn't communicate; she was too judgmental, too critical, didn't listen, was not an available person, was narcissistic and self-absorbed, controlling, and held her daughter too tightly to her.

- One woman said her mother was not a good mother to her while growing up, but that the woman had redeeming qualities that she showed later in life.

THE MOTHER–DAUGHTER RELATIONSHIP

A mother is a very powerful figure in the life of a girl. The competition between father and son is not any more full of conflicts than the one between mother and daughter. Sons talk about wanting to outdo their fathers, and fathers may be tough and controlling in an effort to keep their sons from succeeding at that goal. Men are expected to explore, achieve, and no one sees it as a betrayal to tradition if the son of a shoemaker doesn't take over his father's shop and becomes a surgeon instead. Men compete, first with their fathers and then with other men, and that's a given in their lives. Women compete a little differently and face a different kind of competitor: their mothers.

Mom is the one you bond to, the first person to approve or disapprove of you. In this century, we're not expected to be near-clones of Mom but nevertheless to resemble her to some degree in attitudes, preferences, mannerisms, and talents. Unlike fathers, mothers are more difficult to separate from emotionally. The reason is that, whether we like it or not, we identify with our mothers in certain ways and want to please her. This is a strong psychological bond. One patient's mother was described as "formal, overly concerned with what others think, pragmatic, unimaginative, but a good cook." Her daughter was nearly her opposite: outgoing, artistic, more concerned with doing what was right than what was safe, but, like her mother, she had a formal bearing and loved cooking.

Emotionally separating from your mother and becoming your own person can be a lifelong process. If you identify with your mother in a positive way, you have an easier time separating from her. If you deny that you're anything like her by rejecting her—identifying with her in a negative sense—you prolong your bond to her and halt the process of separation.

A positive separation requires two understandings on your part: (1) you believe your mother loved you for the person you were, and (2) she accepts your move to separate from her. You can get stuck at this second point. I've worked with patients who cannot separate from their mothers because separation feels tantamount to a loss. One patient said, "I want my mother's life. I want what she has with my father, but I also want my own identity. I don't completely know what I want yet, and maybe I rely too much on my mother. I know I need her approval." You can hear in her words that there is still the underlying fear that if she acts like an individual, not under her mother's control, her mother won't love her.

No matter how you feel about your mother now—whether you do or do not care about her love today—*you wanted her love when you were a child*. What motivates children is what they wish for, and what they wish for is their mother's love. If you grew up with a clinging, demanding mother, you may become submissive in an attempt to please her—especially if you fear that the consequence of not pleasing her is abandonment.

If you grew up with a neglectful or cold mother, you may give up trying to please her by becoming rebellious and a "smart-mouth." By rebelling, you are really stating that you acknowledge that nothing you do will make your mother love and accept you. Then you may turn to men—most commonly men your mother doesn't (or wouldn't) like, for that approval. Writing your mother off or cutting her out of your life is not that easy. Unless you examine and resolve a difficult relationship (for example, through therapy) and *go on*, you'll duplicate your childhood experience with your mother through other people. If your mother berated you, you'll seek out relationships with men (and with women friends, too) who will also berate and mistreat you. You'll try to get from your choice of fault-finder what you needed from your mother, but chances are you'll be disappointed.

While you're dealing with your separation issues, so is your mother going through her own process of separating from you. She's also dealing with her issues of competition with you. You're ripening; she's aging. You have the world of opportunities ahead of you; she feels hers are limited or at a standstill. It's obvious that mothers are more likely to identify with daughters than sons, and experience their daughters as an extension of themselves. Problems arise when a mother denies her daughter's differences and her right to separateness and instead demands, "Be like me," or, "Don't show me up."

Daughters who perceive their mothers as having no power in the marriage have a different form of the mother–daughter relationship. Some women in this kind of family reject their femininity and join with their fathers in denigrating their mothers. When that happens, daughters identify with the aggressor and develop "attitude"—angry, challenging, or rebellious behaviors toward their mothers and other women in general. The quality of being "feminine" is seen as weak unless it's crafty. With attitude, girls can never allow it to be said about themselves that they're gentle or kind. It would make them vulnerable to manipulation.

When mothers see their daughters as competition for the father, and this is most threatening during a girl's adolescence, the relationship is a minefield of emotions. Mothers who are insecure in their relationships with their husbands may become punitive toward any show of blossoming femininity in their daughters. They become overseers, scrutinizing how she dresses, how she sits, and whether she lingers over a fatherly kiss. Daughters who fear losing their mothers' love may do anything to try to keep it, including developing eating disorders to maintain a boyish body, or putting themselves at arm's length from their fathers. Daughters who make an effort to win their fathers' attention may cause their mother's further disapproval, or rejection. Often a disapproving mother sees her daughter as beginning to flower just as she feels her own beauty and youth fading, and she does not like it. She criticizes her daughter, sometimes cruelly, undermining the girl's feelings of worth and self-confidence.

I've heard so many women say, "My mother was the worst!" not recognizing that they are having a fairly common experience. No mother is ever perfect, and some are not "good enough." No daughter is ever perfect, and some, not good enough, too, but we act out our issues with others in an attempt to finally get some control.

If an existing mother–daughter relationship is troublesome, repairing the relationship may be less painful than you thought.

Repairing the Relationship

- "My mother doesn't hear what I say, only what she needs from me. She's never said she loved me, and only once in my lifetime said, 'Jenny, you're a good daughter.' No matter what I do for her, including helping her out financially, she never says,

'Thanks,' or, 'I appreciate it.' She just complains," says Jenny, age fifty-five.

- "My mother has no idea why we keep arguing. I recently found a picture of a baby-sitter who I was crazy about when I was maybe eight years old. My mother looked at me and said, 'After everything I've done for you, you remember some baby-sitter!' I said, 'I didn't say I don't remember you, I said I *also* remember Anna.' It was like a shot in her heart. She was hypersensitive, and took every comment that didn't include her as an insult," says Sally, age thirty-six.

What did your mother want for you? What did you want for yourself? Does she appreciate and accept who you are? Some of the biggest conflicts with your mother over the years revolve around how these questions are answered and lived out. When Jenny says, "My mother doesn't hear what I say, only what she needs from me," or Sally says, "My mother has no idea why we keep arguing," they are talking about a pattern of relating to their mothers. They are having the same argument over and over again, even if the cause is different. Jenny and Sally both believe there's little or no way to get through to their mothers and thus no chance to repair a fractured relationship. Not so.

Repairing a relationship may have to start with you, the more enlightened person. Repair begins with your attempting to understand your mother's history and how she got to where she is. Just put aside your own needs and interests for the moment and think of her. Your mother does not need to be alive for you to do this. Although an intimate conversation would be best, there are relatives or neighbors, or even her friends, who can help you get to know her. You need to understand her roots, the challenges she did or didn't overcome, and some information about her relationship with her mother, your grandmother. Give her some slack.

"Even when a mother is ill-intentioned, it doesn't mean she

can't give you something," said Janet Fitch, author of the novel *White Oleander*, which was made into a movie. This is the story of a self-absorbed mother who ends up in prison and doesn't understand what her incarceration does to her teenage daughter, who is left to foster care. Sometimes your worst enemy can teach you a lesson that holds for the rest of your life. The lesson is that you can make it because you are alive and well, and capable of shaping your life into whatever you so choose.

And if repairing the relationship is not always possible, there's a concept you can hold on to that can help loosen a painful grip on the past: give up the idea of having a perfect, loving mother and *accept that your mother was good enough to get you where you are today. Accept that you were not a perfect daughter but were good enough to get where you are today, too. Now it's up to you to go farther.* These are achievements. (This, in very large part, is an answer to the women whose quotes open this section.)

The idea of being good enough helps you release the longing for what you *didn't* get from your mother, blaming her for how you feel deprived, and instead appreciating your mother for what she *did* give. It also releases you from the burden of feeling you have failed and the anger that comes from feeling your mother failed. Your mother did her job, however well or poorly, with what she had available to her at the time.

Personally, I thought I had the most difficult mother in the world, but over the years I've spoken to women who've had as problematic a mother as mine or one who was far worse. I never wanted my mother's life for myself. The day I got married and was leaving Brooklyn, New York, forever as my mother's child, she stood in the doorway of our apartment and asked, "Why are you going? There's an apartment in the building you can move into." My worst nightmare had just come from her lips—the apartment below hers could be mine and I'd be entrapped, forever, in her life, not mine. That apartment represented what I felt would be the *end*, not the beginning, of my life.

However, my mother-in-law was quite a remarkable woman who showed me a path that was very different from the one my mother trod. Dr. Leah Hecht Friedman walked down Fifth Avenue in the first suffragette march. She was an elegant working woman. I met her when I was fourteen years old and took her as my psychological role model. My mother, on the other hand, was a woman I felt bound to but did not want to grow up to be like. She was a housewife who apparently once had some workplace skills. I'm told that during World War II, she was a street warden. This news shocked me because I knew her as a woman with no confidence, not a woman capable of clear thinking or able to help people in a crisis.

My mother proved to me that self-confidence can diminish by taking the path of least resistance. Give in, or give up everything except what's necessary for basic survival, and do no more, and you lose your muscle and your edge. I'm not sure why this happened to my mother, but in part it was because of the divorce from my father. In remarrying, she repeated an old pattern that would fail her: trying to change others, rather than herself.

I think I became everything my mother didn't want me to be. Girls were not to go to college, no less graduate school—a woman's career was seen by her as grounds for divorce. Fortunately, I did things in the right order: graduated from college, got married young, and didn't get pregnant out of wedlock, a big deal in the years when I was growing up.

I looked at myself through a magnifying glass to be sure I didn't follow my mother's life. Yet as a young girl I had her temperament . . . a fiery one. I know I'm not alone here. Many of us become, at least in part, what we fear the most—our mother. Yet finding similarities can be healing. I was reading therapist Phyllis Chessler's book, *Woman's Inhumanity to Woman*, in which she unabashedly wrote about her feelings for her mother. She paints a picture of an indomitable, if not traditional mother. Chessler says her mother was the devoted housewife who banished "all spontaneity" from her life and had no channel for her energy other than what she gave to her family.

Phyllis Chessler wrote that her mother was proud of her ability to dominate others. She said she was like her mother, too, in that both of them are quick to tell others what to do—that "my way" is better. "Unlike my mother," she wrote, "I do not restrict myself to my own children. The world is my oyster." How revealing an admission this is for a therapist! She added that her mother had "no capacity to show affection." Ms. Chessler adds, "She was very ambitious, and I used to say she could run a small country, which is exactly what she thought she was doing when it came to her family."

This is Phyllis Chessler understanding her mother, appreciating the story and even reinterpreting how she perceives her, and perceives herself *in* her. She continues with heartfelt affection, saying that her mother's death "continues to bring us closer. . . . She is gone and yet I think about her more now than when she was alive. I know what she would say in any given circumstance. I have come to understand my mother as the one person I've tried to please, the one person whom I could never please and she would say the same thing about me." This is an incredibly powerful statement, an absolutely sensational admission.

Chessler's openness and honesty is revealing of herself, and, in some ways, she's said it for many women. When you lose your mother, you also lose a little of yourself. But when you cut her off, you lose the opportunity for repair.

What's Your Mother's Story?

One way to help repair the relationship is to look at where you mother came from, the circumstances of life she came through before your birth and as she raised you. Her story can help you put your relationship into perspective by gaining compassion for her point of view.

Our mothers grew up in a very traditionally based, far more moralistic society than we did. In fact, the mothers of most of us who were born before 1960, were raised in an entirely different world-culture. Those mothers were trained to be discreet and close-mouthed about personal problems. In our mothers' generation—women who are now in their seventies, eighties, and nineties—open discussions about sex, ambition outside the home, abortion, breast cancer, or even an honest admission of age were considered inappropriate, if not crude and rude.

As a psychologist, I know many women say their mothers find it difficult or painful to talk about intimate problems relating to any of these subjects.

Paradoxically, your mother may be nothing like you, yet she wants you to be like her, to validate her as a woman. If you take a cool look at where your mother has been, you can actually better understand where you're going. The simple psychological truth is that as girls grow up, they absorb and internalize their mothers' feelings about life, love, men, family loyalty, goodness, badness, morals, guilt, and even about getting older. Some feelings you reject; some you retain.

However, this does not mean that you will totally recapitulate your mother's life by understanding her or even identifying with some of her attitudes or feelings. Identification is not duplication. Being aware of how your mother felt forms a foundation for your own free choices.

The only way to heal old wounds is to get a sense of your mother's story and at least notice the pain she is feeling. This pain may spring from an incident she can't even deal with and might want to deny because it was so intolerable. Catherine, one of the women who answered the Mother–Daughter Questionnaire, told me of such an occurrence. "My mother was always detached or depressed when I was growing up, and obsessed with being good," she said. "She was an ace with giving you punishment beyond the crime and making you feel you were like a foster child, only in her house temporarily. She'd talk about her parents the same way all the time: that her mother was an 'angel' and that her father was a 'bastard.' I knew nothing more than that."

Catherine related that when her mother was in her late seventies, the woman stopped eating and was anorexic. Catherine wanted to take her to an eating-disorder clinic to get help for her, but the idea of talking to a psychiatrist terrified her mother. Finally, she asked her mother what was really bothering her, and she learned the truth. "She freaked out," she said. "All those years she'd been holding in memories of a cruel father, who, it turns out, was a violent alcoholic who beat her and her sisters. Once she finally said it out loud, she was better. I felt sorry that she had such a miserable childhood. It didn't excuse her from all those years of treating me badly. But I finally had some empathy for her. I didn't want to hold on to awful childhood memories, the way she had, and just let mine go. She was, after that, just Ma."

Catherine's mother dealt with her own demons by attacking her daughter. By knowing her mother's history, Catherine could see that by trying to help her, she ultimately helped herself. Like humor, empathy and kindness are connecting points to another person. When you address the fact that you know she's tried her best in a difficult life, you can change the relationship and stop hurting each other.

Marcia had a different problem with her mother. "I was aware that wanting to be different from my mother was a wound upon her," Marcia said. Now in her early fifties, Marcia says she and her mother fought nearly all the time, even when she was married and living in another state. "When I was growing up, my wanting to be an interior decorator was as shocking as if I'd told her I wanted to marry a clown and join the circus. My interests threatened her very existence. It was clear to me from a very young age that I'd have to fight to carve myself out of her life and be myself, although I had no idea what that was. I just knew I didn't want to be like her."

After thinking about where her mother came from—the rural South in a time when girls weren't expected to graduate from high school—Marcia put her mother's limitations into perspective. "In some ways, I think she was smart enough to know that I didn't want to be like her, and she desperately tried to keep me home. I know she feared she'd lose me for good if I pursued my dreams in fashion. I just wanted her to say, 'Go with God!' not tell me I'd be damned for going off to art school. On the other hand, she was willful and strong enough to try to make me back down. But I'm like her. Willful and strong, and I made my own life."

Marcia's mother never would accept her as she was, and both women lost the opportunity to know each other better and come to enjoy each other's company.

"I was terrified of my mother, but shared her dreams. She was glamorous, thought of me as her creation, and raised me to be a star, to do what she couldn't do for herself. She gave me a lot of freedom, yet in some way, she forced me to achieve," my longtime friend, the portrait painter Patricia Hill Burnett, told me. Patricia was once a first runner-up in the Miss America contest. Although she said she was raised to be a man's woman, she co-founded the Michigan chapter of the National Organization for Women. Now in her eighties, she says she is still a bit of a geisha.

~~~

Writer Lois Gould also had an ambitious mother. In the memoir, *Mommy Dressing: A Love Story, After a Fashion*, Ms. Gould writes about her fashion-designer mother, Jo Copeland, the "Chanel of America" in the forties and fifties. As much as she admired her mother, so was she intimidated by her. She feared not measuring up to her mother's expectations, a fear that was increased by the fact that "Mom had no visible flaws."

What's interesting is that her "flawless" mother was a self-invented woman, who had had a tragic childhood. Clothing, and the appearance it could create of security, status, and well-being, became her mother's shield from unpleasant realities. Copeland's gift was in designing clothes for women that created a facade—a quality she valued in herself and others. Shopping and dressing create such a facade for many women.

"Clothes were her refuge from the facts of life—and therefore death," Lois Gould writes. While her mother thought "sexy" was good, sex was not, she said, "because for sex you had to take off your clothes." Interestingly, Ms. Gould was surprisingly casual about clothes and had little of her mother's interest in fashion.

Although our own mothers may not have had glamorous careers and were or were not obsessed with appearances, Lois Gould's feelings could easy reflect many of our own. You can read into her story the emotionally loaded mother–daughter competition and the impact of a mother handing down unstated or stated rules of behavior for being a woman. Reject them or accept them, but in either case, they'll have an impact on you.

Ms. Gould scrutinized the hot-button subject of mother–daughter competition. Her mother was angry and jealous when Ms. Gould published her first book, but proud when it became a bestseller. She looked at her mother's history, character, influences, relationships, and emotional needs in a tender and levelheaded way. She accepted her mother's need for white-glove perfection and is proud of her mother's achievements and admires her mother's ferocity in achieving them. Reaching a conclusion about who her mother really was helped Lois Gould make peace with who she herself is in relation to her mother: a different woman with similarities.

Think about your mother and try to answer these questions about her:

- Do you feel that your mother is an angry, competitive woman?
- Did your mother's mother hold her back from a career she wanted or from marrying a man she loved?
- Are you confused about why she insults you?
- Are you doing something that she would have wanted to do when she was your age?
- And, for the final question here, I'd like to quote a British sitcom character who lamented about the lack of mother love in her life. She said, "My mother didn't give birth to me; she just had something removed." Thus my question: Did you have a mother who made you feel she was sorry you were born?

RESOLVING THE HOT-BUTTON ISSUES

- "I grew up terrified of my mother, who treated me like a chronic irritation she couldn't get rid of. By the time I was thirteen, I'd hardened myself against her verbal and physical abuse. When I was thirty-two years old, she called me and asked why 'her children don't like her' and what she could do about it. No words were more shocking to me than if she'd told me she was leaving my father for Sean Connery," says Sarah, age sixty, divorced.
- "Marry a rich man and do what he wants," Jan says her mother told her. "My mother was interested in money and very manipulative and an expert at both. She was unable to make a decision, and if it didn't work out, she'd claim she was coerced into it and blame it on the decision maker."
- "Obey your husband, and don't make waves" my mother said. "But she could have done better by her kids, like telling my dad to stop touching and whipping us girls. She could have loved us more," says Bev, age fifty-seven.
- "My mother likes to embarrass me in front of my friends by im-

plying I was a spoiled or lazy brat growing up, which was never true," says Bonnie, age forty-five. "I'd like to say she's improved. When I was younger, she'd insult me in front of her friends *and* my friends."

"My mother is on me for the men I date. She should talk. My father was mean and cheated on her whenever he could. She stayed with him until he mercifully died," says Erica, age thirty-seven."

Every woman I've spoken to about her mother can recall at least one hot-button issue between them. This is a knee-jerk, stimulus-response situation where your mother brings up an unresolved issue that she (or you) knows will, effectively, kneecap you. She takes aim, fires, and you drop. Or, conversely, you volley and she falls. The hot-button issue always ends with someone angry or in tears. For example, mothers can remind you that you're not married and therefore are an embarrassment to her. Or she may keep telling you that you're not as smart/pretty/popular/talented/thin/rich as your sister. She may complain that she still doesn't understand why you don't teach third grade instead of waitressing by night and trying to be an actress by day. If she's really angry, she may curse you for having been born.

And then there are your idiosyncrasies: You get your mother angry by never arriving on time and not calling to say you'll be late. You visit her for Sunday dinner but spend most of the afternoon making calls on your cell phone, or going to your old room and closing the door. Whenever she offers advice about men or money, you tell her rudely to pipe down and that your life is not her business.

Thus, you feel put down, and she feels used. You feel inadequate; she feels intimidated. She gets you with guilt; you get her back with guilt. You both argue, you both feel bad, and one of you ends up crying.

Can you really defuse these hot-button issues and never have to deal with them again? The answer is yes, by deciding you will not respond as you normally do but will instead change the subject. It can be this easy. What matters is not what you hear your mother saying, but *how you deal with it through reason, not emotion*. The goal is to remain standing with self-confidence, not buckling from the weight of old issues.

What's really happening in these interactions? When I was growing up, mothers had great latitude of expression. The Victorian rule they lived by was some version of "children should be seen and not heard." It made them feel powerful. Before the 1970s, if your mother humiliated or cursed you, that was her right. Whether or not her comments were true, humane, fair, or psychologically damaging, she was always considered right just because she was your mother. Women from that era were more vocal about keeping girls in line through intimidation, and many didn't hold back. There's still some of this rigorous mothering these days, too. It may sound unpleasant, if not horrible in some cases, but it happens in homes all over America.

So this is the fact of life: no matter how old your mother is, or how or when she was raised, she may toss hot-button issues at you to get a rise out of you—with or without witnesses. Bonnie, a patient, recently asked me, "Why does my mother have to humiliate me? I always call her on the lie, and she just laughs and says, 'Maybe I remember differently.' There was no 'differently.' What purpose is there for her to make me feel useless?" Bonnie said, providing a clue to her mother's motives. It is clear to me that she is in a power play. She expects Bonnie to respond as she does—by being hurt, teary-eyed, and then on the defensive. The routine always works, so she always does it. This way, she is assured that her daughter has no power as a woman and is *still* her child.

The psychology of such mothers may not warm you to them, so let me give you another point of view on this kind of behavior: there's a good chance that an attack salves their fear of growing older, a painful truth you have nothing to do with and can't affect. The attack on you even makes them feel good! I'm not saying they plan the unpleasantries or that the need to push you around is even in their conscious minds. They may have just looked in the mirror and spotted another wrinkle around the mouth, and you walked in looking good, and young.

What is it that the unfulfilled mother sees when she looks at you? You remind her that *she's aging and you're ripening*. The aging process brings up a myriad of feelings between mother and daughter that motivates hot-button issues. Mostly, your presence is a reminder that your life is ahead of you, and that hers is behind her—and she doesn't want to deal with that fact at all. Second, it only takes a glance in the mirror to confirm that even if she looks wonderful, her beauty is fading while yours is surging. Your mother doesn't want this competition.

Instead, she wants to keep her daughter an ugly duckling and delay her development into an attractive woman. A patient who wanted contact lenses when she was a teenager said that if her mother saw an article in the papers on contact lenses, she'd clip and discard it. Beth's mother believed that if Beth didn't read an article at home, it didn't exist. It turns out that Beth read them anyway—her best friend would clip them out and give them to her at school. Beth's mother was undermining her and also hoping to prolong Beth's girlhood. She didn't want Beth to grow up, develop into an attractive, pursued woman who would then leave her.

And there's your side: your knowing that the end of your mother's life is unfolding before you, and how that is scary to behold.

Almost every myth or fairy tale with a young beautiful heroine has as her nemesis her stepmother, never her birth mother. *Snow White* and *Cinderella* are classic tales structured like this. It was once considered morally objectionable to suggest that a natural mother could resent her daughter or attempt to kill her or enslave her for daring to be prettier or chosen by fate to have more. You were not allowed to speak of motherhood this way, just as it is not politically correct to suggest that women are hostile to other women.

Therefore, growing up—and even as recently as yesterday—you might have heard an opinion of how you look, via your slightly resentful and jealous mother's eyes. She may well have told you how flat-chested you are, how dumpy you look, how contact lenses won't help a face like yours. She may have scrutinized every pore, and made you feel doubt about your femininity. Perhaps she brought home clothes that were wrong for you, and she may continue to make poor choices for you all your life. Meanwhile, you've been looking at your mother, her style, her way of being a woman, and asking yourself if there's anything about her you would want to emulate.

Playwright Wendy Wasserstein, who wrote the Broadway hit, *The Heidi Chronicles*, once wrote of another kind of "mommy dressing." Shopping with her mother for a dress brought up old battle lines. Her mother presented Wendy with a pink strapless dress with words like, "This is you." Ms. Wasserstein didn't like it, but to assuage her mother, she tried it on. A slightly zaftig woman, her image in the mirror proved her right about the dress. She said she felt "like a piece of Fleer's Double Bubble Gum was looking back at me."

Annoyed with her mother, she told me she said, "Look, this is you, and this is me, and this is the space between us. We're two different people. If you like this dress so much, you buy it!" For all of Ms. Wasserstein's success and status, it appears that her mother still wanted to dress her according to her own style.

There's a wonderful quote from actress Angelica Huston, a woman still known for her aquiline beauty. She said, "I remember overhearing a conversation between my mother and father when I was about twelve . . . to the effect that 'Angelica wasn't going to be a beauty.' My way of dealing with that, even then, was: I'm going to make myself beautiful. I might not have physical perfection, but I'm going to think myself into being beautiful."

This story exemplifies the belief that it's not what you experience but how you respond that matters. Ms. Huston took a remark she was not meant to hear and made it a catalyst to define herself in a particular way, which was to be beautiful. Another woman might have felt, "Oh, great. I'm doomed. Even my parents don't think I'm pretty enough." Instead, Ms. Huston used it to her advantage.

Learning Compassion

"I think it's a classic trick to make you a child again," Sarah said of why she thinks mothers and daughters still have a hot-button issue—that is, mothers use the "sore spot" against daughters, and daughters agree to feel sore. Sarah is the woman mentioned earlier who had said she grew up terrified of a mother who "treated her like a chronic irritation." Out of this very troublesome relationship with very little show of caring and love, came resolution and repair. It was quite a story.

Sarah, who is now sixty years old, grew tall when being a tall girl was more unusual—she was five foot ten when she was thirteen years old, in the early 1950s, when short, pert blondes were the ideal. "I could never walk forty feet without someone commenting on my height," she said. "I always came home feeling hurt and confused." Her mother gave her good advice: to stand up straight, keep her dignity, and don't look back. But now let's flash-forward to the mid-1970s.

When her parents moved to California, her mother wanted to introduce her to the friends she'd made in a club she'd joined. Her mother asked Sarah to change the sandals she was wearing, with a small heel, to flats. She refused. Her mother said, "But, you're too tall." Sarah made a joke and said, "'It will be all right. I don't intend to date any of your friends."

"That night," Sarah said, "My mother stood at the guest-room door and said in a hurt tone of voice, 'I don't understand why you have to wear heels.' I refused to discuss my height and how I dressed, one more time. I said in a very level voice, 'I'm about to watch the eleven o'clock news. If you'd like to join me, please do. If you want to talk about my height or my shoes, please leave.' She left."

Sarah felt her mother was saying, once again, you're unacceptable because you're artistic *and* tall, and someone to be embarrassed by. "Until the night of the showdown, she still believed I could be hurt by height issues. It came to me that mothers might want to turn you into children again, using what they know was once a vulnerable point. It suddenly felt ridiculous to talk about."

All sorts of feelings and motivations go on that we are not consciously in touch with about our mothers. They may not be in touch with them, either. But then the question is, why do you think your mother keeps doing what she does to hurt you? I had another perspective on what Sarah's mother could have been saying to her. Her mother may very well have thought that she somehow was responsible for Sarah being single at thirty. Commenting on Sarah's shoes was an easy lead-in to what she couldn't say: "I want you to be happy, get married, and give up your way of life so I can feel like I was a good mother. I want you to be normal, so look normal and take off those heels." In her mother's thinking, Sarah was a recalcitrant brat who would not heed her good advice. So she started at it again with the underlying message, "Maybe you didn't hear me the first thousand times I said this to help you, so I'll say it again . . ."

What's interesting is that this incident was right on the heels, no pun intended, of another emotional confrontation. "I always felt like I was dodging my mother's wrath for being different or for being my father's favorite child," Sarah added. "She tried to be a better mother later in my life and had no idea of how to do it." You can never say it's too late, because Sarah's mother took a step that changed their relationship. Sometimes the truth helps heal a pained and fractured relationship.

Her mother called her and said, "My children don't like me—what have I done wrong?" This is extraordinary. "She was a vain woman who always believed she was right. She managed to get the strength to talk about the past," Sarah said. "No words were more shocking to me than if she'd told me she was leaving my father for Sean Connery. I said I can't speak for my sisters, but I can talk about my own childhood. Then I'd tell her something horrible that she did, like threatening to pull me from my bed at night and leave me at a children's shelter. Until I was eleven, I'd often go to bed wearing my pajamas over my day clothes, in case she actually carried out the threat. She denied what I told her, blaming my sisters for what she'd done, then calling back a few days later to say, 'If I did *that*, I apologize!' She became a mother who went from criticizing me constantly to being a better mother, in her way. That allowed me to be a better daughter, in mine."

By the time of this conversation, Sarah had let a lot of the past go, with the help of therapy. It's hard for many people to easily give up old grievances. They tend to keep that pain with them for a very long time. It intrigued me that her mother was willing to discuss the past in such a forthright manner.

Other mothers aren't yet willing to take responsibility for their actions and repair relationships with their daughters. Instead, they may bind their daughters to them through negative emotions, like *guilt*. Polly, who is forty, divorced, and pregnant for the first time, is such an example. I reread her responses to the questionnaire and was amazed at how similar the father of her baby is to the description of her mother—hypercritical and disapproving of her. I spoke to her about some of her feelings.

Polly said her mother was the "guardian of her soul," but her mother's idea of "soul" has more to do with dogma than love. Sadly, Polly never mentioned the word "love" once in writing about her mother. "My mother was burdened with being right and could see the corruption in others," she wrote. "All I ever wanted was to take care of myself. My dream was to be a successful businesswoman, have a great relationship with a man, be a great wife and mother." Now pregnant and unmarried, she wants to be with Dan, the father of the baby. He acts out some makeshift commitment with Polly while not contributing any money toward Polly's medical bills nor promising aid when the baby is born. "I always seem to pick guys who I think I can make into who I want and need," she told me. "So far it's not working." But she clings to Dan, hoping he'll change. "And what's funny is that his style of caring for me is very much like my mother's."

This is how Polly feels most describes her relationship with her mother: "I always felt like a cat. She fed me and changed my litter box. Sometimes I was noticed and sometimes I was not. She took care of me to the letter of the law. She took care of the law of mothering, but not the spirit of it. She really doesn't know much about me. She's a better mother when you're needy. She's very controlling and loves it when you give up control to her. I always felt abandoned, and I long for her [love], yet I fear her control and transfer that to guys now. I pick guys I fear but who I'm fascinated by. I guess I want to control them and fix them and change them. I rebel against authority and did that with her."

While Polly believes her mother is very unsupportive of her, the truth is that her mother is dead right in her view of Dan. "My daughter throws her life after losers. My daughter doesn't know her own value." These are the words of a mother who cares enough about her daughter to want her to love herself. But, unfortunately, Polly's mother doesn't know how to communicate positive feelings, and Polly doesn't know how to accept them.

Her mother is not unlike Sarah's before she was willing to face herself—judgmental and remote. And, like Sarah until she knew better, Polly has a hard time accepting that her mother cares about her. "She's very unsupportive of me," Polly insists, really speaking as the rebel child, not the grown-up. "She sees my pregnancy as a mark against her, that she didn't know how to bring up her daughter. She thinks Dan's a loser because he's not making enough money, and because he's a drinker."

Can Polly make her peace with her mother and repair the relationship? Polly would need to ask her mother to forgive her for rejecting the standards by which her mother lived. By rejecting her mother's values, which is how her mother defined herself, Polly seems to have totally rejected everything her mother stands for. Furthermore, Polly would need to tell her mother that it means a lot to her to be a mother, and now that she's forty years old, it may well be her last chance—right or wrong. Her mother would need to accept the apology and view Polly's choices a little less harshly. Both mother and daughter would need to realize that they want the same thing from each other: honest affection and acceptance.

So far Polly is unable to approach her mother and open the discussion. Her belief in a lack of acceptance from her mother still drives her relationship with Dan. He's still in her life, unchanged and ungiving. I'm hoping that Polly will be able to heal the relationship with her mother and finally free herself from the burden of guilt.

Your mother probably tried her best with what she knew, could do, and had available to her. As a daughter, you probably tried your best with what you knew, could do, and had available to you. Repair of some sort is always possible. Try to avoid losing your mother; don't cut her out of your life. When you reject your mother, you wind up removing pieces of yourself and the ability for greater self-discovery.

CONFUSING THE ROLE OF MOTHER WITH THAT OF FRIEND

Two calls of the wild 1960s were, "Never trust anyone over thirty" and, "You're over the hill at thirty." There was even a fashion movement at the time called the "youthquake," based on a growing population of teens and people in their twenties with disposable income. The style was young, and the thinking—once considered revolutionary—was about personal freedom. Many of the people who talked about being dead at thirty are very much alive at fifty-something and in better condition physically than they are emotionally because, in many ways, they haven't grown up at all.

I'm talking about one specific problem: those who have adopted the adolescent ideal of making their children their best friends. It may have evolved from a 1960s "everyone's equal" policy, drawn to an extreme within the family. It has also become a common form of flattery now for a young woman to say her mother is her best friend and for her mother to say her daughter is her best friend also. I know this statement is supposed to indicate the depth and honesty of the bond, but it is an inappropriate bond that can be quite destructive to the daughter.

So many young women tell me that their mothers discuss issues of divorce, or finances, or problems with their fathers, even their sex lives, with them. I understand that a mother in pain may seek sympathy, comfort, or reassurance from her child, but it is too much for her to expect a teenager, or even a daughter in her twenties, to counsel her. When you're very needy, putting a child on the level of a peer usually doesn't elicit impartial advice. A daughter is placed in the middle of a conflict between two parents and is being asked by one to take sides against the other. This is hurtful for everyone involved.

Here is an example of misplaced friendship in the mother–daughter relationship. I was recently at a dinner party of ten women, where a mother and daughter were two of the guests. The daughter was across the table from me, and her mother sat on my left. At one point the mother made a remark about her daughter's sexuality—that Diana liked younger men she could boss around. I felt that was more information I needed to know about this twenty-eight-year-old woman while eating lemon chicken. The woman said, "Diana doesn't mind. She knows what I do in bed with her father."

Interesting, I thought, and said so. It turns out that this mother *and her friends*, both married and divorced, include Diana in many of their social engagements. Since these older women all talk openly to each other, they don't censor anything from Diana. Thus, this daughter knows about the sex life of every woman in her mother's group, including her mother, whom she calls her "best friend." This is totally inappropriate. Diana needs a mother, not a pal. This mother needs to grow up and stop playing the boy-crazy teenager, both in cahoots with, and using, her own daughter as facilitator.

Being a best friend to your child may mean you choose to turn a blind eye to how she may be pushing limits. A patient of mine, a young single woman of twenty-three who is trying to make it on her own, also still socializes with her parents on occasion. Betty told me that her father's friend Rob is always after her when they meet at social events, and it worries her. Rob manages to always stand close to her, asks her to dance with him if the event has music, and makes sure to touch her inappropriately while flattering her.

Betty's mother chooses not to see the danger in the flirtation. She thinks it's cute that her friend's husband finds her daughter attractive. Nor has she spoken to both Rob and Betty about cooling it. This is a kind of immaturity in which she is hoping to relive her sexually active youth through her child.

But the plot thickens. Betty told me that she had a crush on Rob when she was a teenager, not so many years ago, and that it's not a one-sided seduction. As it turns out, what worries her is not that a married man and friend of her father is making advances, but that she's confused about what to do. She's not only encouraging Rob's advances and toying with him, she confessed to having frequent contact with him by e-mail. This lack of boundaries on the part of both of them is a potential disaster in the making.

Let's fast-forward. If Betty has an affair with Rob, her parents will insist, "We had no idea." I told Betty that she's looking for trouble. There's no question where this folie à deux with Rob is going. Betty's playing a game with a man who means nothing to her, but if she decides to have a fling with him, it'll ruin some other woman's marriage. The result? Betty will turn out to be a hated figure in her mother's social group.

Growing up allows you to be a good parent to your child or a wise parent to yourself and have the capability to remove yourself from harm's way!

What I find interesting about the "nice girls" is that when they identify with their mothers, they tend to marry a man like their father. On the other hand, when girls rebel against their mother, they tend to marry a man similar to their mother so they can go back and try to fix that primary relationship. The whole mother–daughter dynamic is then cast in a different light.

When you have a *non-nurturing mother,* you don't believe that anyone else has quite a mother like her, so it's a revelation to find out that many people have mothers critical of them. Many mothers hope their daughters live out the dreams they didn't get a chance to live out, or they want their daughters to do things differently from the way they did them. Sometimes they want to give their daughter opportunities that they don't want. But the biggest issue seems to be that whoever we are isn't right for them, and whoever they are isn't right for us. And this situation occurs with great frequency.

MOTHER'S WISDOM

- "The worst thing you can give a child is the best. Leave her something to strive for."
- "You know it's love when a man makes you feel smarter, prettier, thinner, and safe. If that man is not your haven, then it's not love."
- "The trouble with getting into trouble is that it starts out as fun."
- "All men will cheat. That's it."

Certainly, some mothers are far more capable of giving sound advice than others. But we need to listen to *what they say, and what they don't say, and tune in to what they imply.* I was talking to a friend who said her mother rarely told her anything but to stay clean and be presentable in public. Tina's mother was up at five A.M. to prepare lunch for three children. She was a single working mother who was too busy in the mornings for conversation and too tired at night for any connection other than basic survival. Tina said she "got it" when she was a teenager: don't get pregnant outside marriage, and make sure you acquire good skills for work. Her mother said it by implication, without speaking a word.

Like Tina, we can garner wisdom from how our mothers lived their lives. Tina was also sensitive to how hard her mother was working to keep them together, fed, and safe.

Not every mother has wisdom to give. But there are surrogate psychological mothers out there who can essentially do the same thing for you. I am reminded of my mother-in-law, who gave me my best advice. I first met her when I was fourteen years old, in my old Brooklyn neighborhood. Her influence on my thinking was profound and changed my life. "If you want my son," she said to me, "you'll get an education and have a career." What? She was talking to a young girl who came from a family where only boys were educated. My own mother had no such aspirations for me, and only wanted me to marry right out of high school to a boy with a steady job. *An education*, I thought, as I looked at this well-dressed woman who was one of the first female graduates of Columbia University's School of Dentistry. *If that's what it takes to get her respect, I'll do it. If I don't get her son Steve, I'll get someone like him.* What I wanted at the moment was his mother's admiration. Her advice was good advice then, and even better now.

FINALLY . . .

So many women grow up to become very different from what their mothers wanted for them. That's perfectly okay. Remember who you were with her as a child, where you came from, where she came from, and who you've become. Compassion is the only way to heal a damaged mother–daughter relationship. If you are a woman who can do this, you have a greater chance of becoming a giving and loving person who enjoys her life.

Now that you've read through this chapter and have other perspectives on the mother–daughter relationship, take this opportunity to answer the questionnaire on page 78, as well as the questions I pose about your mother's history that appear on page 92. Your answers may reveal more than one way to strengthen the bond between the two of you.

4

EMOTIONAL HEALTH

Healing the Sore Spots

Not long ago I gave a speech for a group of women on managing difficult emotions—for example, what happens when anger takes over and everything you do, see, or hear seems tainted by it. When I called for comments from the audience, a woman who runs one of the programs for the group stood up and said, "I spent ten years in therapy trying to figure out what was wrong with my husband. I wasted my time and my money. My therapist wanted to talk about me—another waste. The point is that my husband is an angry man. Don's mad, and he'll always be mad. I just have to figure out how to live with it."

Other than suggesting that she take another look at the dynamics of her marriage and who is really angry, I let the comment go. It wasn't the place to dig deeply. Then, about six months later, I gave another speech on becoming an adult that focused on healing what I call "emotional sore spots"—those hurtful responses that get triggered automatically and make you feel vulnerable, outraged, or bring you to tears. Again this woman was in the audience and I was surprised to see her. After the speech, she came over to chat and introduced herself.

"Remember when I said I spent ten years trying to figure out my husband's problem? Well, I wanted to thank you. I finally got it, listening to your speech a few months ago," she said.

"What did you discover?" I asked.

"Only that he's married to a jerk!" she laughingly replied.

She explained, "I've been replaying a fight I had with Don in my head all day. When you talked about being aware of your anger and where it comes from, I suddenly *heard* myself yelling at Don. I was being shrill and demanding, the way my mother used to act with us kids. Now I know why we're always arguing—it's me. Don is married to a sorehead! I'm always ready for a fight. In fact, I'm always looking for one."

In truth, both she and Don were angry because they *each* felt unsure of being loved by the other. Anger had become a way of nonproductive communication. By *denying* her problems, she tried to deaden the pain of her unhappiness by blaming Don for their rocky marriage. By being arrogant and so sure that Don caused all the problems, she ensured that things would stay the same.

Her ability to open up and share her truth gave me a sense of accomplishment and touched me at the same time. It took courage to confront her role in the mix and admit to it. She knew she had to make a decision: *either give up the rage she carried around and unleashed on her husband, or destroy a marriage she wanted to keep with a man she truly loved.* The choice was an easy one for her to make once she saw it. A future with Don meant more to her than turning old "sore spots" into fresh wounds. Although she cannot change the past, she *can* change how she behaves today. That she could own up to a truth about herself after all these years proved she'd come a long way. I knew her life and her marriage were about to improve.

⌒

Think of how much *you* could accomplish in relationships, in your career, or at gaining peace of mind if you could harness anger, denial, fear, or whatever else makes up your sore spots. This is not to say that negative emotions are all bad all the time or that you should not feel them. Negative emotions provide information about what's going on in your world—they tell you that something is out of harmony and could cause harm, loss, or emotional pain. But the danger of letting negative emotions rule your responses is that they do not propel you forward or allow you to function in your best interest over the long run.

Often, the secret to healing sore spots lies in *recognizing them, appraising the situations in which they arise, and being ruthlessly honest with yourself* on why they still affect you.

ANATOMY OF A SORE SPOT

Emotional sore spots are almost always attached to a person or event from the past—they don't just crop up and surprise you. The situations that trigger a sense of hurt may not be the same now as then, but, unconsciously, you've made an emotional connection that brings you back in time. For example, suppose the time is now and the following happens:

- You're twenty-nine years old and living on your own. Your mother's first remarks upon seeing you at a once-a-month Sunday family dinner is always a version of this: "My friends keep asking me why you're not married. What's wrong with you?" The sore spot: you feel as if you've disappointed her. Once more, she is suggesting there is a basic defect in you, and you become defensive. "Thanks for pointing that out," you say. "Your friends will be the first to know when I meet someone."

- A coworker who is generally popular is sneakily underhanded with you. In a low voice, she jabs you with comments like,

"Anyone could do your job," and, "You think you could head the department, don't you?" The sore spot: you know she thinks of you as serious competition, but for some reason, you fear her and worry that she could bad-mouth you and cost you a promotion. Inwardly, you may have a long-standing fear of not doing things "right." You don't answer her.

- You're having lunch with three friends at a casual pub-type restaurant. The waiter serves your friends, then minutes later, serves you last. You jump at him with, "What do I have to do to get food around here? I haven't eaten all day!" The sore spot: you fear you will be overlooked and that your needs are unimportant to others. You feel entitled to your outrage and go on a tirade about how insensitive people are.

- Your husband walked out on you two years ago, and you're still grieving as if it were yesterday. When a friend fixes you up with a blind date, you spend what turns into a short evening with remarks like, "How could I ever trust a man again?" and, "You look like you go through women like a shark through water." The sore spot: you feel humiliated and abandoned by your ex-husband and see other men as potential victimizers.

From where do these sore spots originate? Responses can be traced to any number of situations in your past. Perhaps you had doubts about your mother loving you. She might have been cool and distant to you, never demonstrative emotionally, though good enough at keeping you fed, clean, and healthy. Or she was bitter and disappointed and took it out on you, telling you that you were a burden and "just like your father." Perhaps your father ignored you and made you feel insecure about being loved by any man. Or perhaps either or both parents, being competitive and ambitious, pushed you into situations you couldn't handle when you were young—trying out for the lead in a play, competing for a scholarship or a teen beauty pageant, doing as well as a brother or sister in school.

Your personal history influences how you behave now—an undeniable truth. Personal history makes you uniquely you, but lingering sore spots hinder your ultimate development. While some transcendental philosophies suggest you get rid of all your personal history to reach inner fulfillment, I would not go that far. Fulfillment lies in healing the sore spots and growing up to be the best you can be.

The situations may not be the same as when they first affected you, but they trigger an unconscious and similar response. In a very real way, these kinds of negative events allow us to continue to connect to the past and continue to have a relationship with someone from our past, which is part of why we don't want to give them up.

There are a few things that are true at various times for an infant: being hungry, thirsty, wet and uncomfortable, or having pain. These conditions need no deep analysis: the problem and the solution are obvious. When you're older and cognition comes in, you move beyond wanting simple bodily comforts and begin to want what other people have, or what you think they have. You're tempted, attracted to, touched by, and repelled by any number of internal or external wants. You may have felt deprived as a child and grow up seeking satisfaction through instant gratification now. Or, if you felt deprived, you may recreate the feeling and the condition by living with real lack or never acknowledging that you have what you want. Or you may seek out a person like the one who helped create that early deprivation and try to find happiness in an impossible relationship. So maybe "not having" is a sore spot for you.

The key to identifying and defusing the negative emotions that keep you stuck in the past is based on *a conscious willingness to face the truth*. With consciousness, you can take responsibility for yourself and your future. Blaming others or blaming circumstances may look or sound reasonable, but it will always be a step backward. Too much valuable energy is lost in holding others answerable for your feelings and your actions.

How you respond either keeps you on the road to helplessness and ongoing immaturity or on a path to fulfilling self-awareness and adulthood. People can convince themselves that they're responsible for good outcomes, but not the bad ones. Thus, if things don't go well, others are to blame. For example, Abby, a patient, was never expected to reach beyond what her parents have, so she finds reasons to turn down promotions while complaining about how employers take advantage of her and how hard it is to make ends meet. Carrie said she could never make a smart choice on her own, so always asks people what to do and lets others control her major decisions. She's then unhappy with the results. In both cases, right now, these women feel ill inside, like they've cheated themselves. But because they don't want to be rejected, they hand others their lives. Do you?

Healing the sore spots reveals one great truth in life: you can't change people or circumstances, but you can change how you relate and respond to life and to others. You can never reach perfection or be totally without failings and limitations. But when the sore spots are healed, you're stronger.

WHEN FEARS STOP YOU

No matter how individual our fears, the common thread is that fear stuns us. Depending on disposition and coping skills, while we're fearful, we can feel helpless, paralyzed, hysterical, even shamed, giddy, or enraged. Because of a sudden sense of a lack of control, a fear looms so large that we lose the objective reality of what's going on.

When you come to terms with the meaning of your fears and

how they affect the parts of your life that don't work, you can either hold on to them or go through a short period of discomfort before you are freed of them. I talked about such unsettling periods of transition with a patient who felt trapped in a relationship she could not leave.

Wendy was stuck at a place defined by a misplaced sense of loyalty and, a sore spot, a fear of living alone. Since she had been widowed five years earlier when her husband died in a car crash, she worried about her three-year-old daughter not growing up with two parents. At thirty-three years old, she met George and moved in with him, believing they'd eventually marry. It was affection rather than love that helped her make the decision to live with George, while overlooking his short temper and tendency to bully her. "He needed to feel in charge," she explained, "and so I let him." George had his good points. "He was reliable, he had basically traditional values, and when we first got together, he always encouraged me in my work."

Then he kept putting off their marriage. After two years together, Wendy became someone George couldn't please, and George became someone Wendy didn't like. "All we did was fight," she said.

A major source of their ongoing battles were about Wendy's travel agency. George was a smart businessman, who had helped her build a part-time agency run from their dining-room table into a successful enterprise. George ran a car dealership, and did well, but he begrudged Wendy her success in that business that was basically *her* idea. She began to dread seeing George at the end of the day. Her life, she felt, was filled with emotional pain and a nagging sense of obligation. She ate to ease the stress and gained nearly forty pounds.

What was happening here? By staying, Wendy tacitly agreed to George's bullying. "I'm afraid," Wendy kept telling me in her therapy sessions before ending the relationship. "I'm afraid Becky will hate me for disrupting her life again. I'm afraid to wake up in ten years and see that George is the best I could do. I'm afraid I can't face who I am. And besides . . . no one wants a fat girl. I'm afraid that I haven't got the stuff to make it on my own without a man."

By staying with George, Wendy allowed an enormous legacy of destruction to grow. It finally dawned on Wendy that by remaining in this relationship, she was putting her daughter Becky's health and happiness at stake. Her husband had died in an accident when the little girl was two years old, and the thought of taking a second father from her made Wendy feel guilty and panicky. Furthermore, fears of complicated legal battles over her business worried her, so she stayed with George.

The day of reckoning came. One morning George made a nasty comment about how much weight Wendy had gained. She called him a name. He countered with a cutting remark about his opinion of her business sense and demanded she hand the company over to him.

"Instead of getting mad and hurt the way I usually would," Wendy told me, "I suddenly felt . . . relieved. He expected me to cry and defend myself. But I just had had it with the same old arguments in different words. I looked at him and said, 'You have no respect for me,' He ranted on, but I walked out of the room saying, 'Whatever, George.' I didn't want to hear one more word. When he left the house, I called a friend and got the name of a lawyer. It wasn't easy to leave, but I made it out of there with my daughter one week later. George fought me for the business. That was okay. Life wasn't worth living in that house, in that misery, for one more day."

She had felt confused, ashamed, and on the defensive with George because fear had ruled her. In fact, her fears had loomed so large, she had lost the ability to look at her needs and how her husband's death had driven her to choose George—thinking a good-enough man who was willing to be in the picture and accept her and her child was better than none. Her fears had so overwhelmed her that she couldn't cope with her eating problem with any sense of objectivity. Finally, George pushed her once too often, and instead of hurting her, he *freed* her. Over their two years together, she'd grown, but he hadn't.

"I was no longer afraid of George and what he could say or do to me," Wendy told me. "It was as if I were prying his fingers from around my neck so I could breathe, so my daughter could live and breathe, too." Despite her anxiety about what might lie ahead, Wendy had the courage to act when she finally stopped telling herself all the bad things that might happen if she left. Leaving was a way of saving her own and her child's life.

Mastering Fear

Mastering fear is not just about overcoming situational phobias, such as learning to swim if you fear being suspended in water, or conquering claustrophobia if you fear tight spaces. Disabling fears extend to accepting success (taking a better job offered to you), fear of loving another, fear of having children, fear of walking into a room where you know no one. Mastering fear is about understanding its relation to a loss of control. But the ultimate fear is "of not being," or of death. All other fears spring from this concept in a variety of ways.

Fear can also move mountains and can be the ultimate motivator for finding and demonstrating your courage. When you come to terms with the meaning of your fears and understand why you must not back away from them, you can start to figure out how to turn fearful feelings around to gain confidence instead.

Bolstering Courage to Fight Fears

Wendy wasn't quite sure what caused her to finally stand up to George. Was it reaching the limits of abuse she was willing to take?

Was it finally realizing that she didn't need George to feel complete? Had her self-esteem grown so that she could leave with dignity? "Where did the courage come from?" she asked herself. If a moment of enlightenment is a turning point in growing up, so is a personal act of courage *both a turning point and the act of turning yourself around*.

Courage is not about backing away from or avoiding what you fear, but about mastering it. This mastery begins by recognizing that you feel a loss of control in the face of what scares you, *then going on*. Courage isn't about deadening your feelings so you go into emotional overdrive.

Like Wendy, you need to think about what you *believe* in before you act. Your beliefs are what give you the strength to say, "No," "Yes," or, "Let me think about it." So, for example,

• You need an accurate definition of your values. Values are psychological ballasts, that take the place of sore spots. An accurate definition of your values will tell you which people, principles, or things are worthy or unworthy of your devotion, commitment, or even fear. Once you know all this, you will have the intellectual and emotional courage to fight to defend your rights, your home, those you love, your country, and, in Wendy's case, the business she founded, without any doubts.

• You understand who and what is threatening or dangerous, and you can resist those destructive forces. So, for example, you don't buckle under to, or side with, anyone who diminishes you on a daily basis. In Wendy's case, she had become George's unmoving target. Their sore spot was the business, and who did what to build it and run it. Maybe George was jealous of her ingenuity, since he worked for someone else instead of running his own business. Maybe his male pride made him need to feel superior by making

Wendy seem inferior. Whatever George's motivation, he showed no kindness to, loyalty to, or admiration for Wendy.

• You have the duty to protect yourself and anyone else to whom you've pledged your support or care. You won't back away from being there for others when they need you. On a grander scale this issue involves whatever would compel you to run into a burning building to save others. While Wendy felt compelled to provide her young daughter with a father, she didn't choose wisely. Becky was seeing her mother in a constant state of agitation, anger, or stress-eating, which could do her no good.

• You have the ability to level with others (especially if you feel they are hurting you or themselves), and you can hear what others have to say to you. Truth-telling may be tough, for it takes courage to stop living with hypocrisy and instead live with integrity. You need courage to tell a friend you feel the man she's about to marry has been lying to her. Wendy needed courage to tell George she would no longer put up with his lack of respect for her.

• You can see the virtue in criticism. We may hear critical words as disapproval, rejection, a brush-off, or an insult, but they can be helpful. Whether solicited, unsolicited, or even uncalled for, criticism is something few of us like. A healthy response is to be open and accepting of it so as to evaluate the truth of it, but I'll move the bar up a bit and suggest you *embrace* criticism, both the taking and the giving of it.

When you see criticism as a beneficial experience, instead of a denunciation of your thoughts, looks, or deeds, or as a vehicle to embarrass you, you have an opportunity to improve.

In criticizing others, be sure to "gift-wrap" the assessment; don't give it out cold. Tell others what they need to know in a way they can hear, and bear. Tact, I believe, is as important as honesty—say what you have to say, but say it with finesse.

Most criticism contains at least a grain of truth. After all, if it didn't, we wouldn't get so upset about it. For example: a coworker who is normally cordial to you says in an uninflected tone of voice, "I see you're wearing a lot of makeup today." Is she telling you that you have a poor fashion sense, that you're obviously trying to conceal imperfections, that you look older, or perhaps even that you look good and better groomed than she is and she's jealous.

How do you handle the comment? What's important is not what she said but how you respond. Perhaps you do one of the following: (1) You don't give her remark any value or examine why she said it, but simply respond with, "Oh, I suppose so." (2) You worry that you look clownish, cheap, or unattractive, blowing her comment out of proportion. Therefore, you say, "It so happens that I'm not wearing anything but eyeliner"—another example of the emotional reactivity I spoke of earlier. The lesson here is to figure out the agenda of the person who is speaking and to assess if her intentions are to help or hurt you.

Remember, a criticism is only one person's opinion, and unless you begin to hear the same refrain from many sources, you can consider the fact that it may not have any merit. Then again, it may. Be open to that possibility.

• You can appreciate what you have instead of obsessing about what you don't. In a world of competitive consumerism and changing partners, we can lose the ability to feel gratitude for what we have and only see what's missing. In part, you may fear not having *enough* and compensate by wanting too much.

Consider the difference between courtship and marriage. In courtship, neither beloved takes anything for granted in the other. In marriage, over the years, a spouse can be considered less important *because* he's there and he's yours. This is typical of what happens if you haven't quite grown up. The brilliance of the conquest fades, and you lose your ability to enjoy the man who already shares your bed. It is like always looking over the shoulder of the partner you're dancing with in hopes of spotting a more attractive man.

People who don't appreciate what they have and envy others put themselves on a carousel of a form of greed—traveling in circles and going nowhere. Greed touches on spiritual burnout. It's a trait that needs to be managed and defused or your life becomes a string of disappointments you compare to others' triumphs. When you have such a jaded eye, you believe nothing is good enough. But once you turn away from what you have earned or have been given and devalue it, you devalue yourself.

Once you know what you believe in, action comes easier. Everything you do brings you closer to who you really are—and makes better connections with others a lot more possible.

DENIAL: WHAT IS AND WHAT ISN'T REALLY THERE

Most of us have been guilty of a common behavioral pattern: denial, a form of self-deception. Denial has many faces, but all of them reveal the complexion of someone who has overstepped some psychological or ethical boundary. Denial occurs in the face of a piece of information you don't want to admit is true, either to yourself or to others. Perhaps you found your husband's boss very attractive and flirted with him in a teasing but suggestive manner, then made a joke of it. Perhaps you appropriated a coworker's idea as your own, then told her "ideas like that are always in the air. Anyone can grab them." Perhaps you "forgot" that you promised your husband that you'd go to a party given by a friend of his you don't like. When he asks you if you'll be ready to leave by six, you say, "For where?"

Denial is a powerful psychological force you use to win the reward of being able to conceal or censor something unpleasant. However, the nagging truth continues, no matter how you deny it.

Denial, like its psychological cousin, *repression*, is a defense mechanism meant to protect you from painful experiences and feelings. There's a difference between the two and how they allow us to feel the sore spots. With repression, your ego takes unacceptable experiences and buries them in the unconscious mind. Childhood sexual abuse is often repressed because you cannot process the pain when you're young, so, instead, you "forget."

Denial occurs when you don't acknowledge or respond to the warning signs that something is happening *to* you or *around* you that means loss of some sort. A patient of mine is deeply unhappy because she wants to be independent of her parents' financial support and control. Yet, Judy will not take a full-time job—one that she does not have to love or keep for the long run—to pay her own way. At twenty-five years old, Judy denies her fear of being on her own, without her parents' influence and money.

Another patient reveals that her husband is turned off to her sexually, even though she believes she's a loving wife. Laurie says she desires Art and wants the intimacy, but she denies how she starts an argument with him before going to bed. Finally, after three tempestuous years of marriage, she decided she'd be better off single again. Laurie filed for divorce, and although her husband fought to save the marriage, he quickly gave her what she wanted, figuring it was the best thing to do. Weeks later, Laurie had a change of heart and could not handle the divorce, specifically the idea that Art would ever let her go. She calls and pursues him, wanting to get back together. "How could he leave?" she cries to me. "Why won't you call me?" Her husband is uninterested in a reconciliation and wants to move on.

When you're in denial and make decisions about your life in this state of mind, you can't function properly to get where you want to go. If you're in denial, you're still hiding and not seeing things as a grown-up. When you deny your part in how intimacy is put off track by your aggression or anger, as Laurie does, you can't truly evaluate what's going on. The result: you stay the same, the sense of disappointment stays the same, the arguments are the same, and nothing changes. When you accept the truth, you no longer live within a self-inflicted boundary that keeps you in the past and, ultimately, from achieving real satisfaction.

As a psychologist, I know that one of the real benefits of therapy is that you will hear not what you *want* to hear but what you *need* to hear. This can be difficult to take, however. Laurie and Art have been divorced for two years now, but for Laurie, it happened yesterday. She still feels that Art is her husband and can't let him go, even when he told her he is marrying again. Laurie is a therapist's challenge—she refuses to be honest with herself about what's under all her protests about the divorce and her manipulative, angry behavior in the marriage. She will absolutely not accept that she did anything to cause the breakdown of the relationship. As a result, Laurie is doomed to repeat this scene again.

There are a number of factors you need to tunnel through before you can leave denial behind you and see the light. The depression, anxiety, or stress you feel will be lifted once you remedy those sore-spot issues.

First, tell yourself the truth about what is happening, or ask a trusted friend, relative, or counselor to evaluate the situation objectively. If your knee-jerk response is, "No, that's not me," you know you've hit a sore spot.

Suppose someone with influence in your life tells you you've got a problem with spending and can't pass up a sale and that "no one needs thirty black sweaters or three televisions. Cut up your credit cards and get it under control." It's important that you hear what this person says, but it is more important to know how you feel when it is said. If the statement has a kernel of truth, you feel poked in an emotional wound. You're being told to manage the discomfort of your idea of deprivation. Your response is to keep shopping to fill the "emptiness" and to excuse yourself with, "Don't tell me what I can and can't have."

Everybody needs some way of getting herself out of an uncomfortable situation, to lick wounds and get a breath. The discomfort may be caused by hearing the truth, but it is only the truth that can help us change.

I heard about an interesting exchange between friends, Lola and Tracy, who hadn't seen each other in a while. Lola kept breaking appointments with Tracy, which upset her. Finally, Lola appeared at a lunch they'd planned. After an affectionate greeting, Lola sat down and said directly, "I'm sorry we haven't gotten together more often. I guess you're still having problems with Peggy." Lola was referring to the fact that Tracy's sixteen-year-old daughter had a drug problem and was in and out of rehab.

Tracy wasn't surprised that Lola would find a reason for the broken dates that had nothing to do with her own breaking of them. Instead of getting sucked into a discussion about Peggy, she blindsided Lola. "Peggy's problems aren't why we haven't gotten together. I don't like making plans with you because you always cancel. Frankly, I'm tired of it. The only reason I'm having lunch with you today is to tell you so. You're too much work as a friend!"

Lola was made red-faced by this confrontation. She didn't want to see herself as unreliable, but that was the truth as Tracy saw it. What could Lola say to her friend? She managed to say, with tears in her eyes, "I'm sorry . . . I want to be friends."

If you find yourself in a spot like Lola's, it's always a good idea to have an authentic and open response, such as

"I'm glad you told me that. I wish you had told me sooner." Or,
"I know you would never say anything just to be mean, so I know
    I must be doing something to deserve it." Or,
"I had no idea you felt that way, and I'll take a serious look at it."

Your best visual image at that moment is of a bullfighter who twirls his cape as the bull charges toward him, not attempting to block the bull's onslaught, but gracefully allowing the bull to rush by. The same is true here: let the charging words rush toward you and by you, but not at you for a full body hit. Don't automatically deny what's been said, but let yourself consider whether it could be true. You also might say, "What could I do to help you see things differently?"

Know if you do or don't want the responsibility of the relationship, the job, the promise, the obligation, the deal or the consequences—and understand that it is not terrible to know the truth. If you can take that first step and say, "Yes, that's me," you can take the second step and admit, "I don't like to hear what I say to others played back to me," or, "I don't like that label applied to me. I don't want to be like that."

After you step back, you can step forward. But you can't act when your emotional circuits are completely overloaded.

• Give yourself a week or so to think about your part in a problematic relationship or event. Talk to your adviser again, and try to see the situation from the other person's point of view. For example, perhaps you've worked since your daughter was two years old and the girl, now fourteen years old, attempts to make you feel guilty for not having been home more. Perhaps you say, "What does she want from me? I made her more independent." This may have some truth to it, but it is also a way of denying that you were not there as much as the child wanted. Don't attempt to avoid or dismiss what she has to say, but engage her in a conversation and tell her what was going on in your life at the time.

• The idea is to learn about yourself, take action or amend your beliefs to reflect that knowledge, not punish yourself. Therefore, don't just talk about what you'll change, then do nothing. June, for example, talks about why she overeats and what measures she'll take to lose weight. Then she walks out of the room and decides she'll start the diet after she rewards herself with what she loves before cutting back. Later, she starts another round of enthusiasm for weight loss. June gets oral gratification by talking about diets. For her, it is a sense of fait accompli—talking about dieting gives her an erroneous feeling of accomplishment, and that's enough. And, in a way, talking about weight loss lowers the anxiety temporarily, not unlike a masturbatory act.

• When you face the truth, you know if you'd rather stay as you are or change, or fully believe you should change. Would you rather complain about a situation because you don't want to change your life, even if it were for the better? Is the truth that you don't want the responsibility of a job, but would rather be supported? With denial, it's easier to say, "I've been out of the market too long, and my skills aren't current," or, "My husband doesn't want me to work," rather than the rarely stated, "I'm afraid. I don't want to have to get up every morning and face that kind of commitment." You may indeed be afraid, but there is an underlying reason for that fear that you need to identify.

Bobbi is a good example of someone who wants power but is not willing to do the work that goes along with getting it. She's an extreme example of someone who bends reality for her own gain and, as she admits openly, gets "comfort from denial." The truth is that Bobbi talks the game of denial, but *she knows what she's doing*: manipulating others. You will probably meet someone like her in the course of your life. You make a deal with Bobbi, who promises to do her part, but the terms change, little by little. She doesn't attend meetings, and you wind up doing the bulk of the work. But when the project is done, Bobbi expects full credit for the job.

Bobbi refuses to take responsibility for what she's doing, but she knows full well that her actions are taken at the expense of others. She pretends to be innocent, but she's not: she's treacherous. When you call her on her game, she swears she's doing everything for the business and denies that she's cheating here or deceiving others there. If Bobbi feels rebuffed by her associates, she indicates that she didn't do anything wrong and cries, "Why are they picking on me?" and feels unjustly punished. Moreover, Bobbi fully expects to be forgiven, loved, and asked to dinner by those she offends. After all, she believes she is a good person. She won't change, at least not until she faces the need to.

Bobbi uses her form of denial to protect herself. It's too painful for her to admit that others don't want to be around her. When Bobbi takes something from you, she's fooling herself into believing you want to give it to her *because she's so powerful*. Phyllis Chessler addresses a dynamic like this in her book, *Woman's Inhumanity to Woman*. She says that when you split yourself in two, accepting the "good you" but denying the "bad you," you'll live in a never-never world where you won't see who you truly are and won't understand why people don't like having you around. Women Like Bobbi are angry, and this is how they deal with their anger. They always feel cheated, so they feel justified cheating others.

Bobbi is in her forties and stressed out from not having an "I" in her life. She has long ago lost control of her values. Her seeming innocence when she harms others sugarcoats both her rage and her jealousy of you. But hearing the truth keeps chipping away at her illusions. By denying that she's needy, Bobbi doesn't get stronger and more successful, but weaker and constantly on the edge of being fired, which is what she fears. She wants to be liked, but she doesn't know how to manage it.

Bobbi tries to reshape the world to her own unrealistic thinking, but it's a world even she cannot fit into. It's too bad she doesn't feel grateful to people who call her on what she's doing. Listening to them might give her a real world to live in.

WHEN YOU CAN'T SAY NO

Donna and her husband are having trouble having a baby. The fertility problem is hers. At the same time, she's dealing with ongoing problems with her widowed mother. The stress of both relationships was getting her down, and this was why she came to me for therapy.

Donna, who is in her late thirties, revealed that when she was a teenager, she was a party to her father's numerous affairs. Her father asked her to cover for him when he stayed out. Caught in the middle, Donna lied to her mother for her father. He asked a lot of Donna, but her father gave her and her sister Betty little in return. An alcoholic, her father was a harsh, unavailable parent and husband. Then her mother started drinking.

When Donna was in her early twenties, her father died of a heart attack in his girlfriend's bed. Donna's mother responded to his death in a way that shocked Donna: rather than being happy over the release from a bad marriage to an unloving husband, her mother created an idealized, heroic version of him. Now that he was dead, she talked about him as if he had never treated her badly, never ignored her, never made fun of her or ever begrudged her spending money. "It was like building a pedestal to hold a peanut," Donna said. "It was crazy."

Donna told me that she never had an honest conversation with her mother. Because she was protecting her mother from her father's infidelities and her father from her mother's anger and accusations, she grew up tiptoeing around them. They both turned her from a daughter into a mediator and a confidante. Donna couldn't talk about her father's affairs with her mother or understand why she endured the abuse. Donna believed she bore the heavy burden of responsibility for keeping them together and providing for their emotional needs.

Donna continued with her role of protector and emotional support system even after her mother moved to Florida. Even now, if she cannot take her mother's phone call or get on a plane to visit when she's asked, Donna feels overwhelmingly guilty. She is wandering between the fuzzy boundaries that exist between her and her mother.

When we discussed why she continues to accept this appointed role of protector, Donna told me, "It's all I know."

Donna's mother feared she had a lump in her breast. Frantic, she called Donna, begging her to fly to Florida immediately to take her to see the doctor. This incident served as a perfect starting point for Donna to begin dealing more effectively with her mother. By being conscious of, and controlling automatic reactions to people, you can learn to defuse some of the emotions that keep you bound to the past. *Reason is an equalizer.*

Donna examined the facts around her mother's fears—her condition, her location, and who in Florida could provide the company and caring. Donna's younger sister lived in South Carolina. Since she was geographically closer to their mother, it would appear reasonable for her to go to her mother's aid.

To help Donna finally have "an honest conversation" with her mother, we rehearsed what to say: a clear and supportive statement. It took her a few days of practice before she had the courage to get on the phone and do it, scared as she was.

"I only spoke about what was bothering her now, and nothing else," Donna said. "I told her that Betty would take her to the doctor since I couldn't get there. I told her to get a diagnosis before she believes this lump is fatal. Let's put fear to the side and save our tears until we find out what's going on. My mother was stunned, but okay about what I had to say. I was shocked that I actually could say it all, my heart pounding the whole time."

Normally, when Donna gets off the phone with her mother, she told me, she goes straight for the vodka. An episodic drinker, Donna would get drunk when she had failed to stand up to her mother and say "No," but instead let the woman wheedle and bully her, making her feel guilty. Days later, she'd still obsess over the conversation, feeling the outrage bubble up—anger at herself and anger at her mother for being such a child.

"This is the first time I didn't react to my mother by feeling I was unimportant compared to her," Donna said. "It was the hardest thing I've ever done in my life. I can't believe what's happened to our relationship in just four weeks."

Since that phone call, Donna hasn't felt panicky about her mother and hasn't been drinking to ease the anxiety. I'm not saying that one confrontation with her mother is a cure for her, but she has confidence in her faculty of reason over emotion, and can exercise it. Taking this one step confirms that she has more control, other choices, and some power in her relationship with her mother. There are new and clear boundaries; she's not adding bricks to old barriers. Donna showed a quality called *self-efficacy*—she believed in her ability to act and get through the process by mustering her courage.

As with Donna, when you don't face your challenges, the problems behind them become more challenging. You can make changes to improve your life and still support and care for others around you. It doesn't necessarily take a lifetime to make a change.

WANTING TO HAND YOUR LIFE OVER TO OTHERS

Helen is in my office, alternately steaming mad and near tears. Helen runs a small costume-jewelry company with two employees, one of whom, until yesterday morning, she relied on completely. Nina worked with Helen for five years, running the office the way a good manager would and being reliable 98 percent of the time. Then, yesterday, Nina e-mailed Helen saying she was quitting and would mail the office keys back to her. "I felt like one of those women you read about who finds a Post-It Note from her husband on the fridge that says, 'Good-bye. The marriage is over. Call my lawyer,'" Helen told me, still shocked by the situation and feeling rejected.

Helen was upset because she was left stranded in her own business, not knowing where to find the deposit slips, the order forms, the tax receipts, or the new-client list. It was not a pretty picture in a small but busy office. She'd given all these responsibilities to Nina, never thinking she had a worry. Nina was reliable, likable, and competent. What could go wrong after five years of working together? A lot.

Helen called Nina to get a reasonable explanation for jumping ship without any notice. Nina said she was having a nervous breakdown and could no longer take the pressure of the job. "It shocked me," Helen said. "I took a few moments to let off steam. It was overwhelming and embarrassing because I was standing there pasting skinny strips of new information onto an old order form because I couldn't find where Nina filed them. I can laugh at it all, but the truth is I let someone have too much control over administrative areas. I should have written up a Survival Manual 101 of 'where to find what' in my own business."

When you live or work with someone, there is a division of labor that can change or break down. It can happen in a business, and it can happen in a marriage. Details can start to slip between the cracks of your own obligations when someone else takes over what should be your business. This is also true of wives when husbands say, "Don't worry . . . I'll take care of it," or wives say, "It's not my job to pay the mortgage or the taxes, and I'm not any good at figuring that stuff out." There may be a day when you need to know what, how much, and where it all is.

I asked Helen what she thought had happened with Nina. Her work situation reminded me of women saying, "How come I never saw the signs? How did he fool me? Was I in a coma so that I didn't see what was going on for the last two years?" How good was Nina at disguising her problems so that one moment she's highly functioning and the next she's flat on her face. Helen told me that she saw a lot of odd behavior the previous month that she chose to ignore. "I liked Nina because we were a nice team. I took the fact that she ran to the bathroom every hour and took some sort of pills every other hour or sometimes got short-tempered and anxious as some sort of phase. I knew she was having problems with her son, and maybe she was distracted. I'd simply assure her and say, 'Don't worry about it.'"

Helen says she didn't want to confront Nina because it might bring things to a head—then she'd have to start over again, breaking in a new assistant (sound familiar?). But her being afraid to confront the truth didn't stop truth from breaking through into her world. What she feared was what eventually happened. Sometimes we don't want to confront odd behavior, but the meltdown ensues anyway. With Nina, the breakdown occurred when she overextended herself in installing another software system and failing at it. Helen could have brought in a techie to take care of it, but Nina insisted it was her domain. When Nina couldn't do the job, things blew up and Nina broke down. The failure must have been overwhelming—compounded by whatever other problems there were in her life that she felt she'd failed at, too.

"I feel angry, disheartened, and disappointed that someone could just walk out on me after five years, leaving a message on the answering machine," Helen said. After talking to her, Nina said she'd come back to train someone, but Helen said, "I can't have her back." Having said everything else, what eases the situation somewhat for Helen is realizing how distraught Nina must have been. "Her discombobulation and anxiety are clearly worse than mine." It's very hard to have a good business relationship, and it takes the same kind of work to make the partnership a good one in a marriage. Nobody feels good about being walked out on. Bad endings hurt.

Helen's sore spot is pride in her independence but wanting to be taken care of at the same time. She too easily handed over the running of her business to an assistant. The same thing can happen in a marriage.

How can you protect yourself? Have access to what you need and learn how to do the tasks that provide it. It's important for you to feel that in the major areas of your life that you *know how to take care of a variety of things*. My friend and attorney, Mike Stein, gave me a great piece of advice a long time ago: "You need a credit card and your own team, one you can rely on—an attorney, an accountant, and a bank manager. And you must know that these professionals are working for you."

In every business relationship it's wise to call in an outside audit. Ronald Reagan talked about "trust with vigilance," an idea upon which this country was founded and which also makes sense in a personal vein. Every time we move away from our own personal checks-and-balances system, we get in trouble. If a partner in love or business says to you, "Don't you trust me?" your reply needs to be, "Trust is when you're willing to be completely open. The issue of trust is proven one way or another by action." Either that person will show you that she/he can be trusted and your concerns are needless, or not. The answer is never a debate. It's simple: show me.

Remember, patterns of behavior form the core of our lives. Women have a tendency to give themselves over to others too easily. There is a vulnerable part within every one of us that wants to be taken care of, even if we're fairly independent. As Helen remarked, "Notice that I couldn't get someone to take care of me better than I take care of myself! I was just delighted to fool myself into thinking it was possible. The tough part was that someone I gave a piece of myself to said, 'I don't want to do this anymore.'"

This is where the feeling of rejection comes in. Helen had to acknowledge it. Nina was taking care of the details, but she was replaceable. So are all of us in any relationship. But the issue is not whether or not we're dispensable. There's a bond with a helpmate. The truth is, we depend on people, and within that dependence, we need to be aware that the relationship can change, leaving one or both of the partners feeling hurt.

Women often talk of the men who got away—those who walked or ran and even those who died. These women bemoan their lot with, "How could he do this to me?" Saying this reveals a sore spot. It also reveals that the man wasn't loved as much as he was needed.

Helen finally said, "I was *too trusting* of a business relationship. A friend said, this is why I get hurt and sometimes feel used. It may be true, but I want to walk into life feeling that another person is trustworthy. Then, if that's not the case, I have to be wise enough to nip the association in the bud.

If you're basically an optimistic person, like Helen, you don't have to become cynical or skeptical, but you do need to be vigilant and mature. In the end, Helen found a worthy replacement and has finally put together that "Manual 101—how to manage my office on my own." Her experience was a great lesson in how to live successfully.

FURTHER HELP FOR DESENSITIZING YOUR EMOTIONAL SORE SPOTS

When people ask things of you or suggest ways for you to change, you can find fifty reasons to stay the same. You know what you do and don't want to change. The secret is right there: facing the truth of what will get you to your goal.

The Atkins diet is one of the most successful examples of this idea. The premise of the diet is summed up in one sentence: if you want to lose weight, eat protein and fat and no carbs. Dr. Atkins says it over and over again throughout his books. Therefore, the rule is, if you want to lose weight, no carbs; if you want to play around with the diet, play around, but don't expect the same results. The diet is a change facilitator, with strict guidelines, and millions of people give it a whirl. This is remarkable. The point is not whether or not it's the healthiest diet for the long term, but that Dr. Atkins set up an unbendable rule for change, and you must follow it if you want to experience the promised change.

Of course, making choices in life is not always as clear-cut as deciding to go on a diet. With a diet, the goal is clear: to lose weight. In other choices the goal may not be as obvious, one reason being that you haven't defined the problem or the solution you seek. "I'm uncertain about what to choose, to do, to think," you may say.

Being uncertain about whether or not you can change is okay. *Uncertainty offers promise*. When you're uncertain about something, it opens up new pathways that weren't there when you were absolutely sure of yourself and the permanence of your sore spots. All of a sudden, you make a discovery. You can stop doing what you're doing—shopping impulsively, denying your responsibility in a failed relationship, saying no. Uncertainty can lead to an opportunity to see the world from another point of view that didn't even exist until you said, "well, maybe it's true."

FINALLY . . .

To feel good about yourself, about getting older, about trusting yourself until you obtain a particular goal, you need wisdom. That wisdom is an accumulation of life lessons that allows you to see yourself as a grown-up. It means facing the truths about what must change in your world and taking responsibility for changing them. It means learning optimism and forgiveness. It means opening the door to a sense of peace, comfort with yourself, and the healing of sore spots. Here are some questions to ask yourself:

- Are you aware of your sore spots?
- What are they?
- Do you strike back when others touch them?
- Are you willing to examine why your sore spots are still so painful?
- Is there a sore spot you still cannot get over? If so, when did it start? Can you connect it to a specific event?
- Are you capable of responding differently?
- How do you respond to criticism? Do you feel angry, discouraged, diminished, bereft, or are you willing to hear the criticism "in neutral"?
- Would you be willing to respond to others with a comment like, "I'm glad you told me that about myself. I'll consider what you said."
- When you think about what was said about you, can you honestly say there was no truth in it?
- If the comment is true, are you comfortable about what you see in yourself?
- Are you willing to learn the truth about yourself?
- If you're not comfortable with what you see, are you willing to make a commitment to change?
- What situations make you fearful?
- In relationships, do you see your contribution to new or ongoing conflicts?
- Do you allow emotions to pile up inside and then explode, thereby fracturing or ruining a relationship?
- Do you avoid or back away from conflict, or do others back away from conflicts with you?
- Can you be honest with others?

- Do you appreciate what you have or just focus on what you don't have?
- Do you berate others as a way of extracting more from them, but deny you treat them as you do?
- Do you make decisions by choosing to see the world as you want it to be, not as it is?
- Do you ignore signs of danger?
- Do you believe that taking a risk may result in a better opportunity?

∽ 5 ∽

A NEW APPROACH TO FORGIVENESS

Not Your Grandma's Forgiveness

Several years ago, I visited my father, who lived alone in a small coastal town in Maine. This was a difficult journey for me, since it was one of only a handful of times I'd seen him since he left my mother when I was three years old. Although she remarried nine years after his departure, my mother never truly recovered from the divorce, and I never grew out of a chilling sense of abandonment.

A week prior to this fateful trip, the late Reverend Jack Boland, then minister of the Church of Today, a Unity Church in Michigan where I often lectured, called to invite me to the Sunday service, where author Wayne Dyer would be the guest speaker. Jack pressed me to accept, making my showing up there sound urgent. I'd known Wayne for years, and hadn't seen him in a while, so I happily agreed.

Wayne spoke on a subject I knew all too well: early abandonment by a father—and, in his case, a heartbreaking story. Wayne's mother had to find a job, and in those days, she had no recourse other than to place Wayne and his brothers in an orphanage until she could afford to bring them home. Wayne's anger at his father became a central theme in his life. It was an anger he carried with him and vented in a variety of ways. When he learned of his father's death many decades later, Wayne decided to visit the gravesite. There, he told us in that church that Sunday, he forgave his father for abandoning the family and not meeting his obligations.

"Easy for you," I said to myself. "*Your* father is dead."

Jack knew I was wrestling with the same issues, which was clearly why he insisted I attend. Wayne's message to forgive those who "loved us not" got me bristling. I wasn't having any of it. Forgive a man who never cared about me or wanted anything for me? *Forgiveness was tantamount to letting someone who hurt me off the hook.*

If I forgave my father, I felt I would be rationalizing his behavior—tempering his abandonment and indifference by having empathy for him. If I forgave my father, it would mean I understood the pain he felt in an unhappy and difficult marriage to my mother. None of these reasons meant anything to me. Forgiveness allowed my father to escape punishment. I wanted revenge. I wanted to face my father, see the man in the flesh, with a voice, a body, and eyes I could look into when I said what I wanted to say to him. I had no intention of crying at his gravesite sometime in the future.

I didn't know at that time that seeking revenge was like drinking poison and believing someone else would die.

What did I consider punishment for someone I didn't forgive? The answer was simple: a confrontation wherein I would hold nothing back—an emotionally retaliatory Full Monty. This confrontation would be both assertive and cathartic, allowing me to make my case, inflict pain back on my father, and finally exorcise my anger at him. I'd let him know that nothing could ever be compensation enough for the unhappiness he had caused. I felt he owed me, and I wanted to collect. Somehow.

Here I was at a church listening to Wayne talk about forgiveness, a profound subject, in what I felt was a shallow and trendy manner. His ideas reflected a culturally popular practice that encouraged the betrayed to embrace the betrayer—a touchy-feely apology that was supposed to transform the experience so both people could move on. This is a great routine for television, but I didn't buy it.

At the reception later, I put on my best social face and teased Wayne about waiting until his father was dead to forgive him. If forgiveness was such a good idea, why didn't he seek his father out when he was alive?

I thought about when my own father left—after which he remained only a shadow figure in my life for long stretches of time. I knew where he lived only from the postmark on the $25-a-week child-support payment that he made dutifully until I was eighteen. He never acknowledged my birthday with a card or called to ask about what I was doing with my life. By the time I married, at age twenty, he'd made personal contact with me on only three brief occasions.

In spite of his absence, I continued making an effort to involve him in my life, but he remained aloof. I was a practicing psychologist, a married woman with grown children, and a television talk-show host, yet I continued my fantasy: *someday my father would want to be part of my life.*

Then an opportunity arose for me to travel to Maine to see him, and I knew this was the time to face him. We spent a distant but polite weekend together. Driving me to the airport for my flight home, my father told me he had opened a small stock account in my name. I was stunned. Suddenly I remembered a weekend I'd spent with him many years before. He had given me a copy of his will to read over. "Line D" stipulated that I was to receive his household possessions while he'd left his money to others. I had taken this as another rejection at the time, but now I realized that it might have been a test of my true interest in him and not what he could give me.

I didn't need or want this stock account. I was pleased that he wanted to give me something, but I was wary of it. Unfortunately, it became the weapon that destroyed our already fragile relationship.

The brokerage house sent the statements to my father, who then forwarded them on to me. After months of this circuitous routing, I called the broker and suggested they send the statements directly to me, to save my father the bother of remailing them. They agreed that this made sense.

To my father, it did not. He accused me of being interested only in the $3,000 he'd put in the account. Was he serious? Too shaken to talk directly to him, I called a close friend of his and asked her to tell my father the money was meaningless to me. "I'll give the account back to him," I told her. A few days later, his friend called to say, "He wants you to sign off on the account."

Every encounter with my father seemed to be booby-trapped. I'd failed his latest test. I finally accepted that I could never prove to him that it was a relationship I wanted with him, not anything material. When he died a few years later, I received a copy of his will in the mail—the one he had left for me to read that weekend in Maine, the one where I was named on "Line D." Now there was a codicil to it that simply said, "*Delete* Line D."

I remember sitting and staring at the words. I was surprised that I wasn't really prepared for this final rejection. Now I had to make a choice: drag around the anguish of this impossible relationship for the rest of my life, or cut it loose now and move on! I needed to relieve myself of this hostile dependency and forgive myself and my father. It was time to let go.

Finding the courage to forgive another, or to ask for forgiveness, as the case may be, can transform your life as it has mine.

WHAT IS FORGIVENESS?

My journey into psychological freedom began with my accepting a new theoretical understanding of forgiveness: forgiveness has a penetrating spirit, but it also has a "body"—actual identifiable components that give the process a structure and the power of renewal.

The most scarring experiences in life—rejection, abandonment, exploitation, abuse, and acts of terror—are the superglues that keep us attached to the very people who cause us pain. Hurtful experiences shape and control our feelings and behavior unless there is a true and freeing resolution.

The problem is, we carry these hurtful experiences with us, always seeking an opportunity to undo them. Sometimes we rouse the courage to face the person who hurt us, hoping he or she will repair the damage by apologizing. This rarely happens.

Others of us deal with "those who loved us not," by either severing relationships with them or living with a kind of detente, believing that forgiveness is impossible but that civility is manageable. There are those of us who cave in and forgive others lest we are seen as "bad" people. Some of us never forgive and build fortresses of bitterness that remain impenetrable for a lifetime.

True forgiveness is never a convenient solution nor a magical cure for a deep emotional wound. Here is what it is: *Forgiveness is the ability to release a negative or destructive bond that keeps you tied to a person or incident. Forgiveness heals you when you release your grip on a painful past—it is not about pardoning the offender.* Forgiveness doesn't wipe out any incident, but it does mean you've defused its power over you. The forgiveness I am proposing not only has the power to heal, but it will change your relationships.

What I learned from the experience with my father is that *forgiveness is for the forgiver, not for the one being forgiven.* When you forgive another of his or her debt to you, you are also forgiving yourself for your suffering, your resentments, your anger at not being able to handle your pain, for feeling worthless and for letting others take advantage of you because you feel undeserving.

Not being accepted by the person who rejected or hurt you doesn't make you unacceptable. If someone is looking to break off a relationship, any incident, no matter how insignificant, will end it. When someone wants to maintain the relationship, no occurrence, not even a calamitous one, will destroy it. *Whether or not a person desires you in his or her life has nothing to do with whether or not you are acceptable as a human being.*

⁓

Forgiveness often appears to be something it's not. Many people see forgiveness as one or more of the following:

- A whitewash of past offenses,
- Excusing what is felt to be inexcusable behavior,
- Tolerating continued abuse from someone who is predictably abusive,
- A victim's obligation to seek out and forgive the victimizer, making the victim "a better person," and, in this vein
- An obligation to forgive an offender upon his request so that he can feel relieved.

These "definitions" benefit the offender and have little lasting beneficial effect on *you*, the person who has been hurt.

How we each deal with forgiveness may fall into one of these general categories, but what we all have in common are perpetually running internal dialogs that never quite change their content. These dialogs tend to focus on one of the following:

- Pleading with the offender to make restitution,
- Beating oneself up for having let the hurtful episode happen, or
- Setting up the offender as the leading player in revenge fantasies.

Most of all, this internal chatter becomes what I call "crazy making." The most crazy-making preoccupations are when

- Offenders deny what they've done to you,
- Offenders will not take responsibility for their deeds, and
- Offenders suggest you "asked for it" and that "you're making a big deal out of nothing."

If you choose to forgive someone, it means you can finally relax. When you forgive, you also surrender your resentment and anger and go on to decide what kind of restitution, if any, will work for you. If your mother was brutal and beat you until you were old enough not to take it anymore, what would be just compensation to you now? A heartfelt apology, an explanation of the pain in her own life at that time, and the clear message that she loves you? If your only solution is wishing her equal physical and mental pain for the rest of her life, you will bind her to you with your rage.

To be forgiving, you give up focusing on what is owed to you. You can cut ties with the other person, or not. However, you're not obliged to keep them in your life, or bring them back into your life, unless they prove they are trustworthy and you choose to.

Perhaps a betrayal or crime against you is a lingering presence. You cannot forget, and you seem unable to forgive. Letting go of the need to undo an experience ends a destructive relationship because *it allows you to separate from the act or person who hurt you.* Most critically, *the successful act of forgiving another is the product of a choice—yours and yours alone.*

WHEN FORGIVENESS MEANS CHANGE

When you forgive, you step to a higher ground and recapture your power by *giving grace.* This is one of the miracles of forgiveness.

This spiritual by-product of the true meaning of forgiveness grants you the chance to make changes in how you perceive others. It is a way to make the past truly past.

My friend Tom's story best describes what I mean.

Tom and Patti met twenty years ago in a small advertising agency. They had similar, and ferocious, drives for success that immediately ruled out their ever being a couple. Patti married Hal, a successful lawyer, and a year later had a daughter, Tina.

After two years in a shaky marriage, Patti filed for divorce. "I spoke to Patti nearly every day," Tom said, "and I was always on her side, especially when Hal filed for custody of Tina. I knew Hal would make things tough for Patti."

Maybe it was the combination of life stresses, both personal and professional, but something happened to fracture Patti's and Tom's friendship. "Suddenly," Tom said, "I heard from a number of people that Patti was saying monstrous things about me. She was lying about who I was and how I did business. She was making me look bad."

When he confronted Patti about the rumors, she said she'd been misquoted. It still made no sense to him. He'd been close to her, but she'd repaid the friendship by humiliating him. Tom's decision was to end the friendship, but the betrayal weighed heavily on him— and he fantasized about revenge: maybe giving her a dose of her own medicine by defaming her or becoming allied with Hal. Then the issue of Tina's custody came up, and he had his ammunition.

Patti called Tom to testify on her behalf in the custody battle. "Patti was asking me to stand up in court and swear she was a better parent than Hal," Tom said, "and I was probably the only person who *could* make the statement. But why should I? This woman tried to ruin my business reputation for no reason at all. I turned myself inside out figuring out the right thing to do."

At first Tom felt that helping Patti was an impossibility. Then he decided that the greater issue was Tina's welfare, not his anger at Patti. And that meant Patti should win custody of her daughter.

"I testified, and it was life-changing," Tom said. "I felt good about myself when it was over. I gave up the idea of revenge and forgave her in spite of it all."

Tom didn't forgive Patti in the usual sense; rather, he rose to a loftier state—*he gave her grace*. Here's the difference: in *grace* you give people what they don't deserve—a *pardon*—and you walk away, free of the hurt and the traumatic connection to an offender. Tom gave Patti what she *didn't* deserve—loyalty in a crisis that called for his connecting to a greater good. The act endowed him with a soaring sense of power based on saving a child, rather than spiting a traitorous friend.

Tom canceled the debt. Patti owes him nothing. With such damage to the friendship, there can never be a just restitution— there can only be *resolution*. Tom released his bond to Patti. By forgiving her, Tom won't carry around that sense of betrayal for the rest of his life. If Patti sincerely changes her behavior, Tom can choose whether or not to allow her back into his life, but that will be Tom's decision alone.

We know about this type of forgiveness on a universal scale. One of the more profound voices to speak on forgiveness is South Africa's Nelson Mandela. Upon being released from twenty-six years of imprisonment, he said he harbored a great deal of hatred for his oppressors. But Mandela realized that in order to be a *free* man, he would have to give up the anger that bound him to those who had oppressed him. He cherished freedom more than he needed to cling to the memories of how he had been oppressed.

Mandela's view is profound because it touches on the idea of "forgiving the debt"—a step he took both intellectually and emotionally. If Mandela's jailers "owe him" twenty-six years of living as a private citizen with human dignity and free choices, it could never truly be paid. Mandela "forgave" those who hurt him by following a psychologically healthier path. He turned the tables and eventually took political office in a country that once didn't recognize his right to vote.

Forgiving the debt doesn't mean you have to testify for your enemies, as Tom did, or reconcile the debt as Mandela has. You can even grant forgiveness to those who don't ask for it in words, but do "ask for" forgiveness by their deeds. Forgiveness, however, doesn't mean you have to love those who hate you or that you are obliged to kiss and make up.

A classic example of this involves the scandal of the Olympic skaters Tonya Harding and Nancy Kerrigan. I remember seeing Tonya Harding on a talk show facing Nancy Kerrigan, whom Harding's ex-husband attacked with a bat across the knees. I interpreted that attack as *killing what you covet*, a common terrorist tactic—though this incident was a form of "personal" rather than international terrorism. It was about "killing" the competition.

The eventual outcome was that Harding apologized and an unsmiling Kerrigan acknowledged the apology—and you couldn't help but notice how reluctantly she did so. That's okay! You may need to forgive someone just enough to gain peace in your own soul. You can decide to never have contact with the person who hurt you, and this, too, is your choice.

And how do you begin to address forgiveness with the very real social and political monstrosity called terrorism, whether or not it touches you personally? Terrorism cannot be forgiven in the common application of the word. I believe "forgiveness" must hinge on *disengaging* from any people, anywhere, who commit indefensible acts upon others. Even with the horror of their acts, you find the courage to *accept* the reality of what has happened and know, deeply and truly within yourself, that it is *right* to disengage from them.

To dissociate yourself from their "cause," you'd need to step away from anyone who attempts to rationalize the madness of terrorist acts. You cannot allow yourself to be taken in by the beliefs of those who seek to excuse repulsive acts with a hate-filled platform. It follows that you need to keep an emotional distance from such people and forgive yourself for not seeing the "good" in them or what they stand for. It really doesn't matter if others care about, follow, love, or would give their own lives for a terrorist. It doesn't matter that terrorists may build an orphanage or are known as being devoutly religious.

What counts is that they finance and foster inhuman acts that disprove any claims they make to altruism or piety. You need to reject all such chatter that seeks to get your sympathy. Very simply, that kind of talk is an attempt to brainwash you in regard to your attachment to loved ones and respect for their beliefs, their diversity, and their very lives.

So there is "forgiveness" by disengagement and forgiveness through repair. Both bring a lightening of burdens. In either case, you're no longer a victim—in fact, you're not even a survivor; rather, you're the *victor*. Real forgiveness results in an appreciation of your own life, the only life you can be sure of having. Real forgiveness says that you're willing to risk being hurt again, and if it happens, you won't be devastated.

Most of all, I'd like you to keep these critical points about forgiveness with you:

- Forgiveness is about the resumption of personal power.
- You can't do other people's forgiveness work for them, and no one can do it for you.
- It isn't enough for you to say, "I forgive you." The person who has hurt you must stop the behavior that will hurt you again in the same way.
- Accept that there might *not* be a way to compensate you for a

terrible wrong, or a continuing wrong. *All you can do is disengage from those responsible.*

When you follow the multistep process I outline later in this chapter, it will take you through the healing stages of true forgiveness. And since the ability to forgive depends on your own personal desire, it's up to you to give yourself this blessing.

WHERE FORGIVENESS CAN TAKE YOU

Fortunes have been spent in therapy in an attempt to find ways to be loved by those incapable of love or to force abusers to see the cruelty of their ways and be repentant and change. The mistake is that we go back again and again, seeking water from the same dry well if not from other equally parched, unyielding sources. Too often, the frustration of continuing failure causes further setbacks. This unrewarding repetition compulsion can only cause ongoing emotional problems.

On the other hand, it can be just as damaging to be swept away by trendy thinking that says it's okay to unconditionally grant forgiveness to those who have abused you. Unless you go *through* the stages of forgiveness—which affect you intellectually and emotionally—the gesture is a hollow one. It can further lower your self-esteem and continue to keep you powerless.

Forgiveness can be hard to get to, but when you free yourself from the burden of psychological pain, it is spiritually rewarding. To have a peaceful core is the most important work you'll ever do. It's part of mastering your environment. It's a matter of *acting on* rather than *reacting to* your inner and outer world. And while it takes courage and determination, it is worth the effort, since it enables you to turn your life in a new and free direction.

In making a commitment to the power of forgiving, you begin to choose who you want in your life, as opposed to others choosing for you. Forgiveness is powerful because:

- It provides the route to make the past the past, rather than being tied to it. You can live now, free.
- It reestablishes your sense of control so you can go on with your life.
- It provides a *violator* the opportunity for redemption—that is, an actual confrontation in which there's an overt request for forgiveness and a granting of it. This occurs only if you choose to give the violator this chance.
- If a violator does *not* ask for forgiveness, then you need to *forgive yourself* for any blame you have taken personally for what occurred, and go on. In other words, you accept that life can be less than fair.
- It frees you to act in the world in your own best interest, as opposed to just *reacting* to occurrences.

FORGIVENESS AND SPIRITUALITY

There are a few generally accepted beliefs that get us into difficulty. One has to do with a commonly accepted concept that true love is unconditional. This misconception says that the proof of true love is unconditional acceptance. This is only true when you care for an infant—such unconditional love is necessary to protect a totally helpless child.

Later, when we're all thinking beings capable of judging right from wrong, unconditional love becomes more problematic. This kind of love suggests that no matter what you do, how you behave, how you look, what your belief system is, if someone loves you, he or she will love you in spite of whatever you turn into. In reality, this rarely occurs. Nor is it healthy to aim for.

Another concept maintains that forgiveness is between you and God, rather than you and the person who hurt you or whom you hurt. There are many versions of believing how God forgives. One version would be that God could not forgive my father for abandoning me. It was up to me to forgive him. I believe God can forgive you for sins against God, such as blasphemy or breaking a commandment, but no clergyman of any faith can speak for you and forgive an offender on your behalf. It is up to those who hurt you to ask for your forgiveness from you, and it is your choice as to whether or not to give it.

Conversely, confessing to a "sin" and being told that God has forgiven you does not really make your problem fall away. When you don't make an attempt to correct the misdeed with the person you offended, you have not truly done forgiveness work, and you have a false result.

ANATOMY OF FORGIVENESS

You can transform the burdens of self-blame, powerlessness, and hopelessness through *forgiveness*. Getting to a true state of forgiveness requires that you go through several steps:

1. A willingness to *separate yourself from the experiences in your past* that cause you pain. And, if it is the case, to disengage from anyone who commits indefensible acts.
2. *Knowing what forgiveness means to you* and learning to differentiate between *understanding* the reason you've been hurt and not *excusing others* for having hurt you. That is, you may *understand the life and motivations of the violator*, but you're not

obligated to forgive the violator because of his own problems and/or hardships.

3. If possible, *confront the person* who has hurt you, or make contact in some way to let her know how you feel. If not, be clear with yourself about why you do not choose to do so.

4. *Admit the depth of your anger* toward the person who has hurt you or betrayed your trust.

5. Use insight and reason to *put the experience into the proper context* so you can come to terms with it, thereby freeing yourself from its power.

6. *Forgive yourself* whether or not you can forgive others—or others do not forgive you. When you affirm your own value and goodness, and understand an offensive act does not represent the truth of who you are, you can release yourself from carrying the burden of the experience in a destructive way.

Let's examine these steps one at a time. (Further case histories will illustrate all of these steps.)

1. *Separate yourself from your past life:* This is a healing step that can be used with great success: separate your present self from the *self of the past,* and speak of yourself as "her" instead of "me." Obviously, you don't want to live in this "split personality" mode beyond the exercise. Its purpose is to help you detach what *was* from what *is.*

That is, at one time you may have been abused by a violent-tempered father, but now you are not. "She" was a child at the mercy of a sick parent; "I" can walk away and choose not to fill my life with similarly cruel people.

In the second part of this step, you need to disengage from anyone who commits indefensible acts and tries to rationalize them. Don't let them convince you of their rightness if they are aggressive and destructive people who enforce their beliefs with violence.

How do you disengage from such people and the pain they inflict on others?

First, find courage within yourself to go on and live your life. Second, go through a grieving process for yourself or other victims of such a person. Third, refuse to accept and/or proselytize the values of destructive people. Don't let their hateful values touch you spiritually. And remember this about forgiveness: *you can never truly forgive anyone who doesn't ask for forgiveness.*

2. Know what forgiveness means to you. Differentiate between understanding the reason you have been hurt and not excusing others for having hurt you. Understanding the reason for the words, deeds, or acts of betrayal that hurt you isn't enough. Knowing another's history and what may have caused her particularly hurtful behavior *does not excuse her* for what she did.

People frequently confuse understanding the foibles of others with excusing them. I read an article in *Talk* magazine wherein former first lady Hillary Clinton explained away her husband's notorious serial adulteries. How? She blamed Mr. Clinton's infidelity not on "malice" but on his personal "weaknesses" stemming from a traumatic childhood and child abuse at the hands of an alcoholic stepfather. Mrs. Clinton further stated that her husband lied about his affair with Monica Lewinsky not "compulsively" but "altruistically" to protect her from being hurt by their vindictive political adversaries.

I'm still not sure if Mrs. Clinton actually forgave her husband or is just confusing "understanding" him with "excusing" him. "Understanding" helps you analyze those who hurt you so you can decide whether or not to forgive them. *And they must want to be forgiven.* Making excuses for them means you are protecting them—and setting yourself up again for getting hurt.

Even when you have the answers, it does not mean you need to forgive others. As difficult as it is, sometimes by understanding another person's pain, you get all the ammunition you need to forgive yourself, and—even more healing for you—*to walk away.*

3. *If possible, confront the person who has hurt you, or make contact in some way to give the violator an opportunity to make restitution.* Part of the healing process will be that person's desire to show he is trustworthy now and willing to make amends for the past.

Confrontation provides the opportunity to tell the person how he hurt you, that his actions were unacceptable and must never happen again. His response will tell you if there is a future for your relationship.

While we'd like to believe that a tearful hug or saying "I'm sorry" is enough, it is not a cure-all for solving a rift, especially a serious one, nor may it completely absolve the offender. How do you know if forgiveness is just words? It's up to you to know what is needed. Here's one test: you'll know if you've forgiven someone or not by whether or not you have lingering anger. And if that person says, "To heck with you!" then go to Step 4 (admit the depth of your anger) and then to Step 6, *forgiving yourself.*

Even if a violator has died, or won't talk to you, you can still confront that person in your head. There is, in Gestalt therapy, something called the "empty chair technique." Imagine the person in question in the chair, and start talking. Or send a letter or perform a graveside ritual, as did Wayne Dyer.

When you practice forgiveness in a way that's sensitive to your needs, you give yourself an opportunity to enter a new phase of your life. It's as if you turn the prism of the event just enough to see the same scene from an entirely new angle, so that you can accept it as a piece of a much larger life and then let it go.

4. *Admit the depth of your anger toward the person who has hurt you or betrayed your trust.* For the sake of your own healing, admit feel-

ings of hatred or fantasies of revenge toward the person who has hurt you—but, of course, do not act them out.

Again, for your own healing, do not let the person who hurt you try to diminish the depth of your feelings. Violators will do this by telling you it's a matter of perception and your perception is wrong, or that they couldn't help it and "you're making a big deal out of nothing." Or they may, in an offhanded way, shrug off your hurt with a comment like, "Lighten up."

Sometimes you can only get to a point where you defuse an unbearable pain that someone caused, but the memory of it still has the power to shake you when you speak of it now and then. This is to be expected. Getting to the point of release from a deep emotion takes time. You may find that indifference is a midpoint sentiment. This, too is all right. Once you unburden yourself of the pain and stop feeling it as a presence in your life, you can go on.

5. Use insight and reason to *put the experience into the proper context* so you can come to terms with it, thereby freeing yourself from its power. When you get to this stage, you are close to having *both* a psychological and emotional resolution of the event, not a casual "let's kiss and make up" surface solution.

Insight provides clarity. You can acknowledge what has happened, see what caused you harm, and put the event into the context of that moment. In getting to a resolution, you have this chance to be honest with yourself and give up denial. That is, you can evaluate the hurt and figure out whether or not it was really terrible, or just an affront not worth the misery you let it cause you. And there's another point to consider: you need to clarify and face whether you were hurt because you were powerless to stop it, thereby permitting it to continue. By being willing to come to a resolution, you give up blaming others and instead take control of the power of forgiveness for yourself. You can then see the rest of your life as having potential for good, and you can see the need to reduce the hold of the negative past.

6. *Forgive yourself whether or not you can forgive others,* and that forgiveness will put you on the high road to personal growth and wisdom. When you forgive yourself, you can finally stop obsessing about people and events you cannot change.

By fulfilling this step, you'll know you can, finally, get past a difficult family background, a troubled marriage or relationship, rejection and even cruelty early in your life. Forgiving yourself allows you to accept the responsibility for having been addicted to alcohol, drugs, sex, or letting the years roll by passively. Forgiveness means coming to terms with the fact that you have children you're not necessarily proud of. Forgiveness makes it possible for you to go on after a tragedy.

Forgiving others isn't for everyone or for every event—but forgiving yourself *is*. Forgiving yourself has great spiritual power and is especially crucial in such circumstances as

- When *you* deem an act *unforgivable* (such as sexual molestation of a child or the murder of a loved one) and blame yourself for not having been able to stop it.
- When the *other person is not interested in being forgiven*—for example, when after learning how you feel, the person continues destructive behavior toward you and wants you to forgive her unconditionally without acknowledging that she's hurt you.
- When the person is *dead or inaccessible.*

You must clarify these distinctions for yourself.

When you can't interact with the offender, forgiving yourself lets you work through the negative feelings by yourself and let them go. And you can win the battle by using any of the steps to forgiveness!

Forgiveness makes the process of *growing up* a lighter, brighter, more freeing experience.

FINALLY . . .

Is it time for you to forgive yourself, forgive others, or ask for forgiveness? These questions can help you move on:

- What is your understanding of forgiveness?
- Does your definition allow you to be a forgiving person?
- What kinds of actions, comments, or behaviors do you find unforgivable?
- Are you the kind of person who takes a minor incident and turns it into something major so that you are easily offended?
- Do you believe that others should be asking you for forgiveness most of the time?
- Do you forgive easily?
- Have others come to you for forgiveness and have you refused them? If so, why is that?
- Do you allow yourself to remain stuck emotionally at some past, hurtful moment in time?
- How has that moment influenced your life in terms of forgiveness and how you feel about yourself? Why?
- When you think about these hurtful times, what do you want from the person or people who hurt you? What kind of revenge or restitution are you seeking?
- Could the person (or people) who hurt you ever really repay you?
- Do you believe there's any reasonable chance they can make it up to you?
- Can you forgive yourself for being in a situation where you were treated badly?

- Do you still see yourself as a person who could be exploited again in a similar way?
- If so, what are some of the things you could do to change your perception of being exploited?
- Is it critical to you that you rescue an offender?
- Do you have a mission to make a good person out of someone who hurt you or who is a hurtful person in general? Can you see that this idea may not be in your best interest?
- Do you understand that forgiving the person who hurt you does not protect you from him hurting you in the same way again? Have you thought about what you would do if he did hurt you again after you forgave him?
- Do you feel more like punishing than forgiving someone so that you can maintain a hold over her?
- Does anger fuel your behavior so that you can't forgive?
- If you rehearsed a speech to forgive someone, what would you say?
- If you cannot get forgiveness, what can you do to move on with your life?
- If you want to rebuild a fractured or severed relationship, and your behavior was really the cause of the rift or breakup, can you ask for forgiveness?
- If you cannot make the first step in making contact with a person who's estranged from you, what's really stopping you?
- How much do you really want that person (people) back in your life?
- Would your life change in any way if you forgave someone who hurt you?
- Have you thought about what you would do then?

~6~

LOVE AND RELATIONSHIPS

*A Good Lover Isn't Necessarily
a Good Man to Love*

It was going to be a "girls' weekend" with two of Helen's good friends, women she spoke to a lot by phone but lately saw only a few times a year. Shortly after her divorce Helen had moved from her native Miami to New York City and got a job on a magazine. This weekend, her old friends would be staying with her in her small but chic rented apartment. She was looking forward to spending time with them, shopping, seeing a Broadway show, and catching up on each other's lives.

Helen met Jan and Betsy when they were all reporters at a Miami paper, all of them in their twenties, with dreams and ambitions. They all wanted good marriages, children, and careers. It didn't quite work out that way for all of them. Helen was married for four years before divorcing her serially unfaithful husband, who, she said, "seemed to be confused about which woman to have sex with other than me!" Jan quit her job after her son's birth, freelanced from home, and was happily married. Betsy eventually left Florida for the Midwest ten years ago, when her husband was transferred there. She'd married Don right out of high school as a graduation present to herself, had two children with him, and got divorced days after her thirty-fifth birthday, "another present to myself," she said. Betsy spent the next seven years looking for a good relationship with the right man.

As smart as she is about solving everyone else's problems and being a good mother, at forty-two years old, Betsy remains lost in a dream about which man is "right." She always picks unavailable men and hopes they will become marriageable. There's been a stream of them, and this weekend Betsy told her friends, "Let's talk about men, and tell me if I'm crazy or if they are."

What's happened with men since her divorce? Betsy's first relationship as a single woman after her divorce began with a man she grew to care about. He was an exercise instructor and the best lover she had ever had. Part of his glory, she said, was that in addition to his technique and solicitousness in bed, he was remarkably endowed. This remark prompted laughter from the other women, but Betsy was really talking about the fact that although she had connected so well sexually with this man, she had not connected in any other way—not much of a laughing matter at all.

"I tried to make the relationship work, but it was about sex and not a future together. I knew I had to break it off, great sex or not," Betsy said. "Then I fell for a married man in the middle of his getting a divorce." Bob's guilt about ending his marriage was overwhelming. One morning after he left my house, he went home and reconciled with his wife without so much as a "good-bye." I had to call his office a few days later to find out it was over."

There were other men who didn't click for Betsy, until Charles. He was handsome, bright, making a good living, and ten years younger than she. By now, Betsy was forty, and she thought she'd finally found the right man. Then Charles said he wanted a family—*his* children. With her own two children grown, ages twenty and seventeen, Betsy was firm about not starting a second family. As a result, the relationship with Charles was doomed. She fought for him, but he left her.

"So," she finally said, "this is where I am." When Betsy finished telling the intimate details of her love life, Helen laughed and said,

"Change the names of the guys and a few details here and there, and you could be talking about me for the last five years. Are all men unavailable, or are we doing something really, really wrong?" Finally, Jan, who'd been married to one man all these years, said, "I've got to level with both of you, and don't be mad. Don't blame the guys. You picked them!" It was a simple statement and a profound revelation at the same time.

What came out of Betsy's story—and how the other women responded to it— showed me that women are still struggling with the same kind of relationship problems that bound women to unhappy relationships decades ago. Although Betsy and Helen are both from a generation that went through the sexual revolution, and the feminist movement, neither woman has learned enough about herself to figure out *who* is responsible for her failed relationships: in each case, *she* is. Jan is right, as tough a truth as it is to deal with.

⌒⊃

I hear about or counsel women like Betsy and Helen every day—women with a lot going for them who are still shortchanging or devaluing themselves! Both Betsy and Helen may have been joking and sounding cavalier when reminiscing about their disappointments in love, but I know and they know they're in pain. They say they want love, but whatever they think of as love has been bent out of shape or squeezed into a pattern of finding men who are "boys grown older" who also have unresolved issues in their pasts. Such women then blame men for being who they are while trying to make them into who they're not.

If I take these women's stories one step further, you'll see how something else has taken the place of love and good judgment these days: valuing sex, sensation, status, the default relationship (any man's better than none), and even danger over trust, friendship, and interdependence as the primary measure of a relationship. This theme comes up again and again. By using the lowest common denominator to find a lasting relationship, you can only repeat your past mistakes and wind up in the same place. To allow yourself the belief that sex, sensation, and excitement matter above all, or that any man will do, you have to start out with the false belief that *a man will do better by you than you can do for yourself*. Some women believe this romantic ideal so strongly they are willing to give up their lives to a man. When you believe that a man will relieve you of your responsibilities to yourself, you also expect him to guarantee your pleasure, protect you from the real world, read your mind, know what you want now and the future in exactly the way you want it. Simply, it means you expect and demand more from others than you do from yourself.

You need to realize that *a good lover is not necessarily a good man to love*. When you focus on the physical pleasure a man brings you, he can only do one thing—fail you. Romantic as it seems, passion cannot form the foundation of a healthy relationship.

Know who you are before you choose a mate. Unless you know who you are and let others know, you'll never get the relationship you want. Positive interaction is a basic human need, which is why so many people persevere in their search for love or marry so many times. Positive interaction is the key to a harmonious relationship, and it must be developed and maintained every day in word and deed.

To know who you are, you'll need to identify the patterns you repeat over and over by honestly looking at the type of man you tend to seek. Is it the very man who cannot love you? What might you be doing to sabotage your own happiness?

LOOKING BACK TO GET A BETTER VIEW OF THE FUTURE

"Feminism gave men anything they ever could have wanted," my friend and lawyer Mike Stein said in response to a conversation about dating in the twenty-first century. I thought it was an amazing remark to make, especially from a male point of view.

What Mike was saying was that feminism made life easier for men and shortchanged women. He gave me many examples. "Women no longer ask to be picked up but will meet you any-where—also saving a guy the need to take her home. Women living on their own don't have the excuse, 'you can't come in . . . my parents are home. Women pick up the check and ask you out. If you don't have sex with them, they're disappointed. They'll move in with you without thinking about it too long and take care of your apartment. It's great," Mike said, "Viva women's lib!" We talked at length, and both of us came to similar conclusions about the man–woman relationship that are important to bring up here:

The sexual revolution in the 1960s, abetted and expedited by the birth control pill, released women from the fear of pregnancy. The 1960s were also about releasing women from the fear of sex, connecting to their bodies positively, having orgasms, and, in general, escaping the conformist rigors of the postwar years.

Being sexually enlightened was de rigueur. It was inevitable that the women's movement would grow out of this sexual freedom. But here's what also happened: that we were equal was a philosophy en-graved on the tableau of the times, but in some ways we took on the worst of male sexual patterns, turning them around and using them against men. This is like seeing the graffiti before seeing the panorama. The disfiguring marks spoil the scene. This is true in any instance where there is an oppressor and an oppressed.

It is almost basic survival psychology that the oppressed will take on the worst characteristics of the oppressor. And some women went for it and became equal-opportunity oppressors. The attitude is accompanied by the faulty ideas that every man is wrong when he disagrees with a woman, and that his feelings can be hurt and he can be acidly humiliated with impunity simply because he is a man, not a woman, and leering crotch-and-buns reports were acceptable—even used in underwear commercials on TV. Women allowed hostility toward *what used to be* to pour out in a variety of ways.

So sex, paradoxically, became the new intimacy, but what it did was stop intimacy in its most authentic form. By feeling sexually equal, a woman could ask a man out, choose to cruise for a man in a bar, end up in bed with him, agree to spend the night at a man's house summoned with an hour's notice, and go there on her own—he wasn't even required to pick her up at her house or take her out. It was "have toothbrush, will stay over."

My friend Mike was right. In general, a man became a prince who didn't have to do much in the way of pursuit or seduction. Women entitled men to have what they wanted without their having to ask for the entitlement.

Although Mike was just talking specifically about how feminism gifted men sexually, I think there's more. Young women today grow up in the most highly sexualized culture imaginable, listening to sound tracks with crude messages and four-letter words passing as song lyrics, watching films, videos, and TV shows that stretch the limits of good taste and reasonable behavior for women. They have responded by having sex at younger and younger ages. Some women behave like sexual provocateurs, challenging a man to have sex on demand. There are men who aren't confident in the sexuality that we attribute to them and have a difficult time with a "modern predatory" woman. Women may well have found the most reliable birth control method yet—men who can't perform!

The mother of us all was the women's movement, establishing what women could grow toward. And, of course, it gave us permission to work as hard as a man and achieve in a profession. Inevitably, this freedom meant that women were worrying more about competitiveness in the job force and grappling with the conflicts of being a working woman, wife, and parent. This was historically par for men, who always had to manage work and family life, often sacrificing family relationships for work. Once, women felt abandoned by their career-oriented husbands, but now women were behaving in the same way. But something else has happened to women. We've taken on the worst of male behavior—more women than ever before drink, take drugs, and are arrested for assaults.

For me, the women's movement didn't go far enough. *It taught us how to say yes but pushed no into the background.* It gave us permission to explore the world in ways our mothers never did: It gave women permission to live on their own when they were young and unmarried. It gave women permission to openly pursue men for sexual favors. It gave women permission to say to a man who didn't want to have sex, "Are you gay or impotent or what?"

What about love in this picture? Has it changed as much as men and women have since the 1960s? It depends on how you define love.

HOW DO YOU DEFINE LOVE?

The definition of what women want may have shifted in the last thirty years or so, but what *has* stayed the same is a somewhat confused definition of love and loving. By your mid-twenties, you probably had felt intensely about at least one man, and perhaps deeply enough to enter into marriage or a committed relationship. As divorce has been made easier, more couples have split up. The discontentment of married life has led to less working through of problems and more walking out on them. Therefore, there's a greater chance that you'll be single again by your thirties and into midlife, and be out there searching for love again.

If you've taken care of yourself and allowed yourself to grow, you've developed a stronger identity and greater self-respect. Your tastes have either changed or become refined, and you've learned more about yourself and why certain things went wrong in the past.

Work may have become important to you, even more important than a relationship. Many women dare to go beyond the boundaries prescribed for them and achieve astonishing things—and a few even become heroines in their own lives or role models to others. Yet, with all the worldly achievements, many women feel *defeated by love*, stuck following ideals of passion or status and hungering for an ideal marriage or relationship. The result is an abiding dissatisfaction and a feeling of somehow being cheated.

Why are so many women suffering over being loved and giving love? Part of the problem comes from not quite understanding what love is and how it works. Real love is one of the great achievements of the human spirit. True love is love between equals, a combination of friendship and affection that offers a sense of stability and security. You feel better because of the presence of your loved one, and vice versa. True love is reciprocal.

Unfortunately, the real thing can get lost among the synthetic images of "oneness," and what passes for love often isn't love at all. Love *isn't* mystical, magical, or as fluctuating and unpredictable as the stock market. It's *not* something to be won like a trophy and then abused or neglected over the years. Love *isn't* just the sizzle of passion or heated attraction, isolated from real friendship between you and him, and given more power as a reason to be a couple than it deserves. Love isn't about hot pursuit of the unattainable guy, or about one person surrendering to another. Nor is it about proving you are worth the pursuit of as many men as possible—enough conquests and one-nighters to fill a book of your "confessions."

There's a sitcom character who, in a sketch, once bragged about all the men she'd been with, saying she even had an affair with Keith Moon, one of the original Rolling Stones. When her friend questioned her as to *when*, she recanted with, "Well, actually, I woke up under him in a hotel room one morning." Her anecdote is funny and tragic at the same time and not too far off the histories of other women who use sex as the standard encounter with a man. Consider the story of Janet, a woman whose experiences typify a certain type of misdirected thinking about the meaning of love and the power of sex.

Janet was an acquaintance I saw socially once in a while. I was surprised when she called for an appointment, saying she was depressed. "I've really screwed up," Janet said to me, with a nervous little laugh. "I need some advice, and now." She still had hopes of making a life with a man who would love and accept her. But she had a blind spot—seeking out dead-end affairs and guilt-relieving abuse in order to have a relationship.

This is what happened: She'd awakened in the middle of the night, days from her forty-fifth birthday, with a man called Vic on her mind. She'd been dreaming about him—a surprise from her unconscious, since he had been her first serious relationship and the first of her two husbands.

Janet was divorced twice by the age of twenty-eight, and she lived with another man while she was in her early thirties. Vic, her first husband, was ten years older than she, a banker whom she "worshiped" at first. Ambitious, Vic worked long hours, leaving her alone too much. Janet found herself getting bored with him, which turned to anger. When he was home, he was controlling and critical of her. She was twenty-two years old at the time, and wanted a husband whose blood pulsed for her as much as it did for his deals. "I didn't have the fortitude or whatever it took to be a devoted company wife. I wanted *love* to be the payoff, not status," she added. "I felt like an accessory, something he brought to company functions, placed on a chair when he got there, then picked up again on the way out."

Janet left him after two years, having met her second husband. Janet believed Doug would be different. He was a carpenter and furniture maker, boyish, fast, and funny. But six months into the marriage, it was over for her. Doug wasn't up there with the stratospherically tough or controlling Vic, but quite the opposite: short-tempered, petulant if he didn't get his way, and demanding of unconditional love. "I think he wanted a mother, and I'm not the motherly type. I couldn't manage the relationship and how he would always set me off-balance, insulting me and making me laugh at the same time."

Vic's wasn't the only ghost that visited Janet before dawn that day. She told me she began adding up the men with whom she'd had affairs and, what shocked her now was the number of the one-night stands. Her past made her laugh and cry at the same time. All she knew today was that her love life hadn't brought her where she'd thought she'd be by her mid-forties—sharing life with a man she could trust and who wouldn't try to change her. Was this too much to ask? Apparently it was, yet she could not figure out why she was still alone. She wanted me to tell her my thoughts on what "went wrong."

When she sat across from me in my office, Janet was a little self-conscious as she began to speak. She lifted her takeout container of coffee and said, hoisting it to toast them, "Here's to all the men I've loved." Her eyes filled with tears as she continued, "Where are they now?" I asked her what exactly she thought about these men and what she had wanted from them. Her answer was revealing: "I probably had sex with nearly every man I ever wanted. Most of those guys looked good enough, but I didn't love most of them. Most of them didn't love me. It got to be about being wanted. Having sex with the guy every other woman wanted because he was rich, cute, a big shot of some sort, or known around town as a good lover. It's hard for me to admit that I wasted my life running around, just to prove something. I never wanted to regret my past."

Although she spoke of herself as a woman worthy of the best men, her behavior signified a woman who devalued herself, giving herself too freely and diminishing what that giving meant to her.

Casual sex is never about love, and she knew it as she took her clothes off with each man. She told me at another session that she believed that "sex was a form of love the way that food is a form of love. The physical intimacy made me feel desired and even temporarily protected. Chocolate cake doesn't do that. Even when the guy would get up off my bed and make an excuse to leave, I knew I'd probably never see him again. I always felt bad, even if I didn't really like the guy and thought, 'Good riddance!' But in a few days, I'd go out looking for another man."

Janet was stuck in a pattern that pretty much guarantees poor relationships. She was bored with and intimidated by her first husband, bullied by a passive-aggressive second husband, and running from love after that. Janet probably wanted love to last with Vic or Doug or a few of the longer relationships she'd had with other men, but something else happened. She never knew how she felt about love, so when it came her way she suffocated it, bent it out of shape, turned it into power plays, or tried to squeeze it into a mold that could never contain it—pure sexuality.

Like Janet, some women forget what matters in a man's character: the stuff that lets you exult in real friendship and cherish long-term connections. This cannot happen if you convince yourself a man has qualities he may not have and construct fantasies about him. And it may never happen if you don't believe you have anything to offer a man besides sex, especially if you've never tested yourself out in a long-term relationship.

Primarily, a good man tells you who he is and demonstrates it truthfully by his behavior. He doesn't sell himself as foie gras and turn out to be baloney paté. A good guy is neither a frog nor a prince. He need not have fifteen minutes of fame, the ingenuity and money-making capacity of a Bill Gates, or a reputation as a sexual philanthropist, always ready to give. What makes a good man to love? It begins with your definition of love. Before looking at the man, examine your ideas about love, being loved, and giving love.

As you go through this chapter, you can ask yourself these questions about what you think about relationships:

- Do you want someone who'll take over your life even though you insist that you want to be independent? Does making decisions for yourself scare you?
- Do you feel you have to stunt your emotional and professional growth to have a man in your life? Do you hide your ambitions and desires from yourself and others?
- Do you suggest to a man that you believe one thing while actually believing another, making yourself less or more *just to suit his criteria?*
- Having once been hurt or victimized, do you seek out other victims? Do you believe that two wounded halves make a whole? Are you interested in saving a man, changing a man, or being his love nurse?
- Do you want a man who'll introduce you to the world, then hope he'll *give* you the world?

If you answered yes to any of these questions, the chances are good that you select men who seem accessible, tantalizing, appealing, easy to take in daily doses, but who may be ultimately wrong for you. These are the men who plug in to your weaknesses, promise love and protection, but keep you wanting. If they do anything, it is offer false comfort with empty promises.

The psychiatrist and theorist Harry Stack Sullivan said that with real love, the needs and satisfactions of another are as important as your own. Real love is a delicate mix of many things and goes through a number of stages.

LOVE AND ITS STAGES

Ask a woman who's newly in love how she feels, and her responses will focus on ecstasy, oneness, fullness, "coming home." Speak to a woman who is newly wounded by love, and you hear about agony, loss, bitterness, confusion, and blaming. Question a romantic on a mission to find the right love, and you'll hear about rapture, surrender, adventure, and conquest. Probe the mind of a cynic who's been deeply hurt at least once, and you'll discover theories about the myth of love, about the supremacy of lust or work, and how they substitute for connecting to another human being, about how love is a psychic weakener and the heart's main function is to pump blood, not create emotional havoc. Love contains most of these elements at some time when you've opened yourself to the experience.

Falling in love may seem magical, but it can be analyzed. Fyodor Dostoyevsky wrote insightfully about the conditions of love in *Brothers Karamazov*. He said, "[F]or love in action is a harsh and dreadful thing compared with love in dreams. Love in dreams is greedy for immediate action, rapidly performed, and in the sight of all. Men will even give their lives if only the ordeal does not last long but is soon over, with all looking on and applauding as though on the stage. But active love is labor and fortitude, and for some people, too, a complete science."

Researchers would later do what he predicted: analyze the feelings and see how they fit into "stages." The first stage, the *ambivalent* stage, is composed of passion, focus, pumping hormones, and magnetism, or "chemistry." This is the stage of great passion and high intensity because of the newness of the relationship, with the edge of anticipation in seeing him and the sense of urgency if you don't. Heightened sensations run the gamut from passionate to obsessional in the first flush. Feelings are primal—this is the man you want, and you feel it, yet it frightens you.

You have an immediate connection to this man, in life and in your fantasies, because he's attractive in a way that matters most to you. In fact, this is where your fantasies about love are at their most potent. You imagine what it would be like to be with him all the time, you write his last name after your first name, you wonder how he is with money. The mental pictures keep you wanting more.

Dr. William Glasser wrote in *Reality Therapy* that the faster two people decide to commit, that is, the quicker they fall in love, the harder the impact, the higher the high, and the hotter the flame, the quicker the relationship will burn out. So passion, anticipation, intensity, and urgency may get you together but may not keep you together. And even if the flame is high and hot after more time together, this introductory step can make you vulnerable. For one, the heated attraction can turn into instant intimacy and get women into all sorts of trouble. The attraction fools you into thinking you've found your match. A sense of "rightness" shades your thoughts about him, and you believe he's a good man to love. Some women get stuck in this stage, craving newness with man after man and overvaluing passion and anticipation in relationship after relationship. This describes my patient Janet's problem and her lifelong issues of "getting bored" with men and seeking sensation to prove she has feelings.

The urgent state of loving doesn't last and will sputter and change over time. Life trickles in, event by event, your need and his need, and dulls the glittery illusions that come with romance. In the mix of this next stage, perhaps one wants control while the other makes unreasonable or even indefensible demands a partner won't accede to. Partners each want something different from life, and neither will compromise. Tempers flair, a partner drinks or cheats and proves irresponsible and dishonest. You feel as if you're out of love, and you fear abandonment.

To recapture the bond, perhaps you start pressing the man for what he once gave you or more of what he has given little of—assurance, attention, interest in your life, gifts. You may feel needy and dislike how he makes you feel about yourself and him. Right about now, you try to remember the first moments of passion, to recapture the bliss, the high, of falling in love.

Love will now move to another stage, in which *exploration* allows you to search out similarities of interests and discover what you have in common. You discuss values and standards. You exchange life stories in vivid detail.

During the next stage, called *revelation*, you test your partner on how much intimate knowledge you can exchange with him and still feel safe. Can you tell him a secret and not worry about being betrayed or feeling humiliated? How does this man you care about react to stories about your past? How much can you tell him, and how much does he ask you about yourself? Because of this semiconfessional stage, you become more vulnerable and begin to worry about losing him. This is when you're likely to feel the pain of real rejection.

Revelation is a sensitive stage in the development of love, since this is where doubts arise. Ambivalence shows its two faces and can loom large. You waver between wanting to free yourself from the man one moment and feeling a heavy, urgent, and abiding need for him the next.

The revelatory stage opens up to you the realness of the man, how he truly copes, what he thinks about money, what he wants from a woman, whether he's reliable when you most need him, whether he's a man of his word or a man of empty promises who goes off and does as he pleases. You learn whether or not he has personal standards you admire. You will certainly learn if he has set the bar for what he wants from a woman at so lofty a level that you could never please him. When you exchange secrets or intimate feelings, you'll hear if he talks about himself directly and honestly, or if he's guarded or makes you guess about his former relationships. This guessing game is a love trap many women fall into.

At the same time, you'll be letting him know how he measures up to your standards. You, too, need to be direct, not vague, manipulative, or game-playing. As Martin Seligman said in his book, *Authentic Happiness*, when you want something from someone, tell him what you want him to do, *not* what you don't want him to do. It would be unfair to punish your partner if he has to guess what you want, then when he tries to please you, you stop him by saying, "Too little, too late."

So the ambivalent, exploratory, and revelatory stages have important benefits: They each in their way present you with the challenge of figuring out what you want from a relationship and whether or not you want it with *this* man. Everyone experiences ambivalence and doubt, and these feelings should not be considered signs of failing in the relationship. In religious orders, such ambivalent and revelatory experiences are tests of faith. Are you called to this vocation or not? The same can be true for getting through these tests of learning how much you really care. This is when many relationships fizzle. Are you willing to commit, and can you do so with a pure heart? Love can't endure on romantic ideals and won't thrive when one person is in control of defining the terms of the relationship.

Love needs maintenance, attention, discussion, scrutiny, adjustments, and confrontation. In the final stage, *union*, you need to be kind to yourself, kind to your partner and ultimately, willing to look at the quality of what you've contributed to the relationship. This is when you'll know if the man you've chosen is just a good lover or more than that—a good man to love.

Out of these stages, the following will happen mutually:

- You don't have to surrender your life to a man or keep a running score, but you give generously and freely and interdependently. You feel that you're part of what makes his life good, and he feels the same about you.
- You know you're okay on your own, but you're enhanced by the man you love because he brings out your okayness.
- You can accept the fact that the man will change, you will change, and both of you will change the relationship. Change does not mean an end, but adjustment and adaptation.

- When you love, you can tell a man that you appreciate him, that you enjoy him, and you happily invite him into your life.
- You can plan your future together and know what you want over the long run. You can keep a good sense of humor or reasonableness about setbacks, trials, and the inevitable grievances, hard times, and even tragic moments.
- You accept each other's idiosyncracies and don't demand he change to suit you. When you talk about what bothers you, you take note of his and your responses. If the response is, "That's your problem," you may have chosen a man who sees the relationship as his and the problems as yours.
- After the rush of passion, you can sustain a level of pleasure and acceptance of yourself and the man in your life.
- You can get up every day and look him in the eye and believe you've chosen to be with him voluntarily and feel good about being there. If the words get stuck in your throat, you talk it out immediately with him.
- With love, you know the feelings of being the lover and the beloved. And you may like the active role of lover more than the passive role of the beloved.
- Most of all, in love, your union adds up to three. Together you create an entity that's greater than the sum of its parts. You can maintain your uniqueness as individuals but allow an easy, natural interdependence.

THE PATTERNS THAT KEEP YOU SEARCHING FOR LOVE

I found this quote in philosopher Søren Kierkegaard's work, *The Sickness Unto Death* and thought it was apt and wonderful: "[For] the self is the thing the world is least apt to inquire about, and the thing of all things the most dangerous for a man to let people notice he has it. The greatest danger, that of losing one's own self, may pass off quietly as if it were nothing; every other loss, that of an arm, a leg, five dollars, a wife, etc., is sure to be noticed."

It may be one of the toughest things to admit to yourself—that you don't know who you are and how life raced by you. This thought begins to suggest what "losing one's own self" is all about. One way that happens is by repeating the same destructive patterns in relationships. A second way is by making the same destructive choices in men while hoping the next version of the same type of man will prove you've been right all along.

Here are the stories of two women who reveal why things aren't working for them.

- "I thought I was smart by getting together with straight-arrow, solid Ben, who'd take me away from the lunacy I grew up in," says Fran, age forty-two. "Ben was sweet, but I thought, 'So what.' I wound up making a big mistake by leaving him and marrying a man I thought was sophisticated and courtly, but he's one of the world's meanest men. Where do I go now?"

- "I want a man who can afford the best and that's what I always wanted," says Rita, age thirty-five. "My husband doesn't earn enough, and I'm home taking care of the kids, so it's up to him. He's threatened to cut up my credit cards and close my checking account, but they're just threats. He threatens to leave me, but he doesn't. I just go out and spend what I want."

While these women each have a different take on what relationships mean to them, they are both talking about the same thing. Thus, to restate one of my original points about loving, *unless you know who you are, you cannot know who is right or give yourself to that person*. The women just quoted may sound like women who know who they are, but they're stuck in the past.

Let's go back to Fran and her "mistakes." Her problem was that after marrying a decent man who loved her and who treated her well, she mistook their relationship for a lifetime sentence of boredom. She was smart because in her first husband, she *married a man who could take care of himself* and be giving. If we talk about her biggest mistakes, there are two. The first is that she believed she wasn't worthy of being loved by a good man. The second big mistake was not letting a man do nice things for her. My advice is that *if you want a man to do things for you, let him*.

In therapy, Fran saw that what she found exciting in a relationship was chaos and threats of rejection, which she had experienced in her family as a child. Her second husband answered all her internal insecurities and gave her chaos in the form of a raging temper. Fran even suggested that by marrying someone nice and finding him boring, she might have been engineering her life to wind up, again, in chaos. "Harry manipulated me with his anger, and I would do anything to make it go away," she said. "I actually believed I'd have the power to make things different, the way I had power with Ben. I ignored all the red flags before we married. Harry didn't have any friends, with all his charm. I should have seen that he was an angry person and it wasn't me making him angry, but by the time we got married, I didn't think I deserved anything better than him."

Fran admitted that she was lonely and fearful when she met Harry, and he made her feel like she belonged somewhere. She's still lonely, but she's decided to stay in the marriage. "I tell myself it may not be forever, but what can I do?" she said. "I sacrificed my first marriage. I was immature and had ridiculous illusions."

Fran didn't know when she had something good. When you know what's precious, you will protect it.

In Rita's case, her spending money is a toxic formula for keeping the marriage together, if on the edge of contention. It is what their relationship is about. But in talking to her, it's clear that Rita doesn't want to hear about real solutions yet. Although Rita's kids are in school, she won't get a job, even part-time, and buries herself in excuses, digging in deeper every day. Rita is an angry woman who's taking her rage out on her hardworking husband, Mark, who brings in a respectable $50,000 a year. All he wants is for Rita to live within the limits of his income, and to not make him feel inadequate by telling him he's not good enough to earn what would please her. But she continues to shop and put them in debt.

Mark threatens to stop the means to her spending—credit cards and a checking account—but in his weakness, he cannot do it. If he did, it would be the first step to end their dance of marital death. Of course, Rita could not function as she does without the complement of Mark's neurosis. That's why when one person gets healthier, the relationship goes awry unless the other makes changes, too. Rita wants Mark to do for her what she refuses to do for herself.

There are women who set things up in relationships so that they never have to do more for themselves, and then they complain, feel deprived or victimized, or like Rita, are angry that they're not being taken care in high style. The question is not, "Why didn't I find a man with greater earning power," but, "*Why won't I do what's necessary to rectify the situation? And, What is stopping me? And, What is the name of the obstacle?*" The answers will vary. Maybe it's because you fear going back into the job market and don't want to be rejected. Maybe you really *are* lazy and unmotivated and expend a lot of energy in the process of sparing yourself the truth.

Above all, you're always looking at this question to answer: who am I? If *you* can't answer that, then you can't expect a partner to plug into your truths and please you. Mark may believe he knows Rita as a demanding woman who confirms his greatest fears about himself: that he's not good enough as a man. Rita has Mark pegged, and uses his fears against him. She's saying, if I spend $70,000 a year, maybe you'll be man enough to meet it. But it's Rita I'm most concerned about. She isn't willing to admit what she's really about. It was something she needed to know before getting married.

You have to know yourself before you form a relationship. You need to know how you take risks in life, how you succeed and fail. You need to figure out what you are like, how things work for you, what your standards are, so you can say, "I am . . ." and complete the sentence.

The best answers aren't what may sound like the text in a personal ad, such as, "I am a 32-year-old blonde who likes BMWs and walks along the beach." These preferences matter, but you need to go deeper and pull up an answer that talks about you in an *internal sense*. Men and women both get screwed up in relationships because they play "let's pretend" and "this is how I'd furnish my dream house" instead of being real. When you're real, you're able to say, "I am a woman who has a strong sense of my values and standards," or, "I am someone who has experimented in a number of ways to see what is right for me," and so on.

You can't tell the truth unless you know what your truth is. If you lie to yourself to protect yourself, you'll never know the real "I am . . ." By knowing who you are in every sense, you can start to match yourself up to the right man.

Passion Is Not a Marital Right/Rite

Sex is the most powerful drive you have, and if you learn how to control it, sex will enhance, not sabotage or destroy your life. What you feel and think about sex in general, the meaning of sexual pleasure in particular, and how sex increases or decreases your sense of power is brought to your bed. Sex, though, is not a marital *rite*, meaning a kind of holy observance on a designated day. You can't produce mutual sexual satisfaction by saying, "It's Saturday. Tonight's the night." And neither is sex a *right*, meaning it is due you.

Harnessing the power of sex is about controlling the impulse to seek sexual pleasure for its own sake. Rather, sex has a purpose beyond the orgasm: to help create and sustain a relationship with your mate. Sex, then, becomes the celebration of a relationship, not the basis of one. Harnessing the power of sex means you know the difference between affection and love and its more libidinous counterparts.

Sensual pleasure energizes us and possesses the ability to take us to another plane of consciousness. Without an emotional connection to another, sex itself becomes the connection—a habitual need for release and, in some cases, an addiction. When you're a sex addict, you feel empty without your "drug," fearful that you won't find a partner to satisfy you. You use pleasure to run from life and from your spiritual needs rather than incorporating it into life.

Just because sexual passion fades, it does not mean that the marriage is a mistake. For most of us, that heat exists for a fairly short period of time, usually a few years. The more you get into the relationship, the more baggage arrives or appears. The amount of time you spend together and how sure you feel with each other can turn up the sex or turn it off.

A patient told me that she was having a crisis of conscience regarding a desire to cheat on her husband.

Carole has been married for four years to a lawyer who works long hours in his quest to make partner at his firm. This leaves Carole alone a lot most evenings. To fill her time after work, she started going to the gym or meeting her friends at singles' bars. She began a flirtation with a bartender and starting going to the bar at least twice a week to see this man.

"I want to have an affair with Phil," she told me. "He's everything my husband isn't. Sexy. Macho." Everything Carole told me about Phil assured me this was a destructive relationship for her. Where could it lead? What was the point? I asked her, "how does it sound when you say to yourself, 'I'm a married woman who's having an affair.' Does it go along with your mysterious self, the sexy girl who moves around from man to man? Do you feel sorry that you're married to Ted?" If she does have an affair with Phil, Carole will very soon find out who she is and how she feels about adultery.

The next week, she told Ted they had to spend more time together. He said he'd do his best, though his job is very demanding and his time is not all under his control. He asked her to be future-oriented, promising her a great life together once they get through this phase.

I love Carole's honesty, especially with this confession: Passion ruled. She'd gone to the gym, then came home to shower, dress, and meet Phil at the bar. As she was changing, the phone rang. She saw it was her husband on the Caller ID and she didn't pick up. She could feel the struggle, but she went to the bar anyway.

When Carole got home, still unsure about starting an affair, but turned on, her husband was home, in bed. She didn't tell him she'd missed his call but that she wouldn't have gone out if she'd known he was home. He explained that he'd tried to reach her, that he missed her, and he'd stayed up to see her.

Carole told me, "I was grateful that I hadn't done anything with Phil. It was so tempting. I can see myself pulled to him, but I want my marriage to work. I shouldn't go back to the bar." She's right. Going back to temptation is one way we are all called by desire. Staying away is one way to not let it overcome us.

Interestingly, Carole's husband didn't question her about her whereabouts. He opened the conversation by talking about his trust in her and by saying he loved her. Ted didn't say anything to provoke guilt or start an argument. But what he said did stir Carole's internal measurement of what the relationship meant to her. Although Ted may not be as attractive as the macho bartender—who is all fantasy and no reality—she's still attracted to him. This is a matter of how you reframe your perceptions and desires. If you see the bartender with buff body and tatoos as a sexual action figure you want some action with, then a studious, slim though athletic professional man with glasses may not be as glamorous. But he's still the right guy.

I thought it important that Carole didn't turn Ted into a bad guy by pushing him to the wall because he's not home enough. She was delighted with herself. "I knew I'd hate myself if I started fooling around with Phil. I'm just glad I controlled this gypsy in me. I have to keep a cork on her!"

Giving Bad Boys the Boot, not the Booty

Bad boys are a big theme in my practice among women who find them irresistible. These are men who are serially and powerfully seductive sexually, emotionally unavailable, dangerous, or are con men. Their effect is beyond flirtation. Feminism has done nothing to deflect the damage they can do if you let them into your life. If bad boys leave you with anything, it is scars.

Some women know better and have trained themselves to resist bad boys. Eileen said, "He stood a little too closely and oozed the charm all over me. I wanted him, and made a decision." This doesn't sound threatening, but her response took courage. She'd gone to a restaurant with two of her friends. After they had been seated by the maitre d', this man approached them and stood around, coming on to her *and* her friends. One of the women remarked, "He's really interesting and exciting. We should draw straws to see who goes after him." Knowing what would happen if she stayed around to flirt with him, Eileen did something she'd never done before when being turned on—she walked away. As she left the restaurant, she said to herself, "This place isn't good for me if he's a regular. I can't go back there."

We could say, wouldn't it be better if she'd stayed at the table and ignored him, leaving her friends to play the game? In other words, wouldn't it have been better to prove she was stronger than his sexual appeal by desensitizing herself? And how could she have been so sure that he would even ask her out? How does she know who this guy really is? Eileen *did* know this guy was bad for her, and whether or not he was interested in her was beside the point.

This charmer reminded her of men in her past who attracted her in a flash. She had given that up. It was very interesting that she made the decision to remove herself from his presence and be sure that she would not get involved with him. This kind of fortitude is part of what it takes to change, to walk down a different path by letting insight and instinct guide you out of a destructive repetition compulsion. The leaving is easy when you recognize that it is less painful than getting involved again. You may feel a loss, but you've taken on the responsibility to protect yourself and move on.

Bad boys come in all styles, as do the women who get involved with them to tame them, change them, or reform them. They rarely succeed. These men inspire heightened feelings, even feelings of love at first sight, but they are not good men to love unless the reformation willingly comes from them. It's more likely that such a woman will offer herself up to a bad boy thinking she can rescue him from his own demons. When you talk about wishful thinking, you can place this rescue fantasy in that category. The deep belief such a woman has is, "If I do this for him, he will change—he will appreciate me, he will love me, and he won't leave me, because this is how I'll change his life. I'll understand him as no other woman has, and he will love me forever because of it." But rescuing a man over and over is enabling him to stay the same.

Rescue fantasies sound noble, but they shift the responsibility for his behavior from him to you. They keep you from confronting him with a question like, *"What are you going to do about your problems?"* Instead, you are helping him out or joining him in his folly when you tell him he doesn't have to make an effort. You want him to think you're wonderful. This keeps him down. Maybe he's chronically unemployed, so you support him. He's an alcoholic, so you start drinking with him. He's a womanizer, so you look the other way and defend him because he comes home to you. This behavior drags you down.

Rescue doesn't allow him to grow or become more. If anything, it stifles growth. You can even fear for him. Laurie tells me now that she worries about Matt, her ex-husband, by whom she is now pregnant. Matt has always run around on her, and he has a gambling problem. When they were married, he was abusive to her when he lost and less abusive when he won. Between winning and losing, he'd have his moments of being affectionate and caring. Yet, she'd defend him in his worst moments by saying, "He didn't mean it." Laurie would set up standards for him, he'd promise to abide by them, and he'd forget them the minute her back was turned.

Matt not only has a gambling problem, but after an ugly fight with his boss at work, he was fired. He was out of work for six months, during which time Laurie gave him money when he asked for it. Finally, he demanded $5,000 as a final "loan," promising he'd never ask her for money again. She said, "I got furious and told him no. I promised myself I wouldn't give him another cent. He *has* to find a job." Then a month later, she buckled in and cried, "I feel so bad for him. He's depressed. I'm afraid he's going to get drunk one night and die in a head-on collision."

Laurie says it's her sense of loyalty to a man she loved that gets her to write a check, even though it makes her feel used. This is beyond loyalty. There's some secondary gain she gets from Matt's continuing to ask her for help. He plays it as if he cannot live without her, flattering her that she's the stronger one. Having hooked her, he goes to the next level. He tells her it's her obligation to help him since she never really believed in him. Matt really is a little boy, and bad.

Rescuing him may make Laurie feel temporarily more desirable, confident, powerful. She fools herself by saying that without her, his life is on a barbed edge. The truth is that she's afraid that if he asks for help and she says no, Matt might be forced to live without her, and she might be forced to live without him *in that role*.

Despite all the love she gave him in their marriage, one morning Matt said he loved her "in his way" but that he didn't want to stay married to her. At thirty-five years old, she reluctantly filed for divorce.

Laurie had begun to adjust to his being gone, when four months later, he called. Feeling needy and still in love with him, she went to his apartment and stayed the night. Laurie was hoping for a reconciliation, but she was in for a surprise. Matt wasn't interested in starting over, but something else started: she got pregnant. So at thirty-six now, she will soon be raising a child alone.

If there's a moral to the story, it's that if a bad boy casts a spell on you, blink and break it. If you're drawn to a mission by an irresistible force, or feel pulled by a deep stirring, it's trouble, not love. In the bad boy's thirst for excitement, people are only receptacles he can drain.

Bad boys are charismatic and experts at finding women to charm for their own pleasure or contempt. When they put their hands on you, they make you feel like the miracle creams that are supposed to take ten years off your life overnight—transformed by a dream come true. Miracle creams don't exist, and bad boys rarely stick around without leaving some damage. Buying into either illusion is costly and unrealistic. This is giving your body and soul to a man with a serious character disorder. You'll never get what you expect—capturing the wild beast. Like Eileen, you're wiser to walk away before you get hurt.

Figuring Out How to Get What You Want Instead of Walking Away from It

How many times have you given in when someone said no to something you wanted. There went your dream. It happens when we're kids and parents want one life for us while we want another. It also happens in marriage. There's an event in a patient's life that explains what I mean.

Jean runs a successful business in town and finally has a loving, comfortable relationship with her husband of thirty years. But, as she will openly tell you, neither was easy until she figured a few things out about herself.

"I love being an adult, and I'm sad that it didn't occur sooner. I came out of what I think of as a self-absorbed coma when I was forty. But I still wasn't a grown-up. I was a bird who had broken through her shell, picked her head up, and said, 'Hey, there's a world out here I don't know about involving others!' What awakened me was celebrating my fortieth birthday. It shook my world."

Jean said she once viewed thirty years old as the end of her young adulthood, and the decade that followed was filled with conflict. She was learning her trade at someone else's shop while struggling with the many roles she was playing: going to school at night to learn about business and management, having a full-time job, raising two children, and being a wife. Her husband was building his own business and had very little time at home for real interaction. She said, "I felt that no couple was so unaligned and crossed in every possible direction as we were." But things would change.

Jean started out believing her life would be perfect. Her adult life began when she left her childhood home in San Francisco when she was twenty years old. Within the next year, she graduated from college in June, married in August, got pregnant in October, and gave birth to her first child in June. They eventually moved to Cleveland and rented a little house. By the time Jean was twenty-six years old, she had two children.

When I asked her about the good parts of the relationship with her husband Pete, she said that one key developmental moment was "learning how to bargain reasonably with him, beginning with our house." This is what happened. Pete was not making much money those years except to meet the overhead. Jean was working at a boutique, paying for whatever else they needed and banking a little. Then she saw a house for sale, walked through it, and saw that the back lawn was a field that led to a lake. She had to live there. "Pete was thinking of houses in a lower range," she said, "but my instincts told me that spending twice his limit for this lakeside house was the smart thing to do. I knew that God wasn't going to make any more lakes in this town and that the value of the property could only increase."

Pete said the house was wonderful but they couldn't afford it. Jean presented her argument by saying, "We can't afford a vacation in the near future and buy a house. So instead of my quitting work, if you buy this house, I will guarantee the mortgage. Interestingly, she never intended to have a career but rather to be a full-time wife and mother. They figured out how they could make the sale work, and did. The house has become her dream house, since they've remodeled it to meet their needs over the years.

Then there's Pete's side. A good man, he realized that Jean had more expansive dreams than he did. He had to think about it, but his decision was to not hold her back or resent her for reaching beyond what was "good enough" for him. Instead of insisting that they live according to his budget, he was willing to go along with her and buy the house she wanted, finally, enjoying what she brought to the marriage.

"When I look back," Jean said, "I love that I could be decisive, take responsibility, and stick to my agreement. I didn't take no for an answer but figured out how to make the deal work in a grown-up way. Most of all, I know that life is too short for perfection."

That's a great line: *life is too short for perfection.* She's not perfect. Pete's not perfect. Her marriage isn't perfect. As psychologist John Gottman said, you don't really "solve interpersonal problems; you learn to manage them." This is wise. Instead of locking in to preset roles, Jean and Pete came to a compromise that ultimately changed both their lives for the better.

Living Together Robs a Man of Being a Partner

As trendy as it has been for the last thirty years, living together does not audition the marriage, serve as a training ground for a permanent relationship, or guarantee monogamy. This has been the surprise result not only to researchers doing the studies on the subject, but to the thousands of women who have cohabited with men.

It may sound plausible, but living together does not do what women thought it would do: smooth down the rough edges and let you see if you could make it together. Recent research has shown that attitudes of the couple diverge as the woman is serious about playing house, but the man isn't. He's still an "I" instead of a "we," and living together doesn't transform him and make him one half of a de facto couple. He stops at that point in the partnership and hasn't really made a commitment. However, he has all the expectations that you've made known to him. He'll let you play it out, and because women are the way they are, you'll probably go along with this one-sided commitment.

If you don't want to get married, you never have to make a commitment. But if you want to get married, living together is probably not a good idea. Even women who have taken on a male-lifestyle pattern—devotion to work first rather than the home—can lose out by living with a man. A good job doesn't make them invulnerable to being hurt. What happens for women in cohabitation isn't fair from the getgo. Women are the ones who will provide the groceries, decorate, see that the house is cleaned, and organize their socializing. The man may have opinions and even make the final decision, but he is only playing boyfriend while paying half the rent.

Living together is not a true partnership, no matter how nice the guy is. If you do cohabit, be sure that you know your legal rights. You don't want to come home after work and find that the locks have been changed and all your stuff is locked inside.

Whoever He Is, You Won't Die Without Him

Here's Ginny, divorced from Fred after twenty years of marriage, still torn by his leaving. Fred immediately started dating a woman he worked with, and they took off for Cancun over the Christmas holidays—their first time away together. The trip was life-changing. Fred went out for a run, came back to their hotel room, and collapsed. He had had a small stroke and had to be hospitalized. Fred's girlfriend called Ginny's eighteen-year old son, Kenny, to let him know about his father's stroke.

Kenny wanted to fly down to see his father, and after he discussed it with Ginny, they left together. In Ginny's fantasy, Fred would be vulnerable; he'd need her and would realize what a mistake he'd made by divorcing her. With Kenny completing the picture, they could be a happy family again. She held on to this fantasy so strongly, she believed it had almost come true. Then she and Kenny walked into Fred's hospital room and saw him lying there with tubes and IVs attached to him. Sitting by his side was a slim brunette who was making him laugh. They were holding hands. Ginny exploded.

She went to Fred's side, asked him how he was, and then told his girlfriend to get out and go home. Her anger escalated until she and the girlfriend got into an unattractive cat fight on the ward. Ginny insisted on seeing this woman as the *other* woman, as taking her possession, and of having no right to be there. Of course, Fred is not expected to be faithful to an ex-wife, but Ginny would not let him go. Fred told Ginny to leave

What's interesting is that Ginny is in other ways levelheaded and not delusional. But she believes only Fred can make her feel like a woman. Ginny's a dynamic businesswoman whose life exemplifies one of those great American dream stories. She grew up in near poverty in Appalachia and moved to Detroit when she graduated from high school, moving in with an older married sister. Ginny married Fred at nineteen, and had Kenny a year later. By the time she was twenty-four, she was on her way to great financial success in an import business that she started on her own with a loan from a family friend.

As shrewd as she is in business, so is she foolish, impulsive, and obsessive about love. When she came back from Cancun, she told me about the hospital incident, a telling tale of her obsession for Fred. Weeks before he took that trip, she dropped by his house on a Sunday afternoon. Fred was trimming the hedges, so Ginny parked in his driveway and got out of her car ranting, "I call you, and you don't call back. Why don't you pay any attention to me? What's the matter with you!"

This is not rational behavior for a basically reasonable woman. Her problem is that she is still married to Fred in her mind, and she cannot cope with the reality of his being gone. These rages make Fred feel disturbed, sick to his stomach, angry, and, at all times, wanting to flee. Unfortunately, Fred has *his* weakness for Ginny and he feels sorry for her, for leaving her alone. "He tells me it's time for me to go on with my life," she cries to me, "but how can I live without him?"

In truth, Ginny will have to live without Fred because Fred has moved on. Her only two choices are to move on herself or continue to rail against reality.

FINALLY . . .

It's always wonderful to hear a woman talk about loving a man and learning that love comes out of self-confidence. So is it always sad to learn the opposite. The truth is that when a woman is needy, she'll seek out a man to provide her with something she feels is missing in her—a strong sense of self, power, and the ability to deal with the world. Being a grown-up means being able to distinguish between need and love.

Ask yourself the following questions to clarify what you think and feel about intimate relationships.

- How do you define love?
- Has this definition of love changed over the years?
- Is there anything about your experience that proves this is a good operating definition for a fulfilling life?
- Do you feel the same sort of intense feelings with trouble or drama as with love?
- Does your definition of love include liking the person? That is, do you hear yourself saying, "I don't like him, but I love him"?
- Do you use sex early in the relationship to "get it out of the way"?
- Have you ever been in a situation where you couldn't say no to a man even though he wasn't good for you? If so, what did you believe you'd get out of that relationship?
- Can you accept caring and loving gestures from a man without being sarcastic or wondering if he has ulterior motives?
- What's the biggest ongoing conflict in the relationship you're in now?
- How can you finally rectify this conflict?
- Do you expect a man to know you even though you don't know yourself?
- Do you expect a man to give you what you won't give yourself?
- What do you see as the basis of a committed relationship or marriage?
- If you are in a committed relationship and have not had sex in more than six months, what is going on between you and your partner?

- Are you still attracted to the bad-boy type and believe he can change for you?
- Are you trying to prove your worth by getting some sort of commitment from him?
- Do you seek perfection in a man, and if so, how must he show that he's perfect?

7

GETTING REAL

*Rolling with Life's Punches and
Landing on Your Feet*

While on a lecture cruise around Africa a few years ago, I met an amazing man. He was working on Robbins Island, the single-level cement-block prison where Nelson Mandela served seventeen of his twenty-seven years for treason. The island is now a landmark tourist attraction. The prison, although closed, maintains photographs of its most famous inhabitants in many of the cells. Since I wanted to pay homage to Mandela, I joined a group being ferried there when our ship reached Capetown.

The man I referred to was the tourist guide who took us around. He had been a political prisoner at this very site for seven years. This man had a peaceful radiance about him that attracted me, and we got to talking. I asked him what allowed him to get through the rigors of jail with such a peaceful demeanor. He told me, "I took a vow along with Mandela to be one who stood up against revenge."

Here was a man who'd lived in the dehumanizing environment of apartheid all his life. In the world outside, he'd survived the prison of racial discrimination; inside and incarcerated, he fought for dignity. By knowing Mandela, he discovered that his *real self* did not live by the codes of hatred. When the prison was closed and became a museum of human political history, he took the job as guide—as a free man who had once paid the price for speaking publicly about the injustice he saw and fighting for the right to say it.

So many women struggle to free themselves from a prison of their own or another's making, and they search for the keys to who they really are. This guard's story was stirring in the context of the society that made him. He'd been forced to live in a prison made by others, yet he safeguarded his beliefs and his standards. He never allowed his oppressors to touch his inner self.

His words made that trip really precious to me. In its way, meeting him affirmed for me that his *unsaid* message is universal: you control what you think, what you say, how you feel, and how you behave. The greatest gift you will ever have is your life and how you view it.

Getting real is a big part of growing up—actually, it is a lifelong process in which you are always clarifying your beliefs. When you get real, as this man did, you give up revenge fantasies (a part of forgiveness), and relinquish the need to refer to the past for answers. Most of all, *getting real means you can roll with life's punches without feeling singled out by "fate" to be handed less than you deserve.* This is a life-changing state of mind.

Life *isn't* all a result of our own choices, but the one choice I'm sure you *can* make is to start on a journey to "what can be" rather than relegating your life to "what might have been." The best journey is when you know what is happening inside you and around you, call it by its rightful name, and face it. You only have today. "Eternity is now," Joseph Campbell said in a discussion with Bill Moyers about the meaning of life. "The experience of here-and-now is the function of life," he continued. "If you don't get it now, you don't get it!"

What matters is appreciating your life, living it to the fullest. The process of getting real is one sure guide to test what's meaningful to you. You can do this by defining reality, asking yourself the right questions, and working out some sort of doable plan that lets you follow through and moves you forward.

STAYING IN TOUCH WITH REALITY

Reality may tell the truth, but whose truth? We're all eye-witnesses to life, but each of us sees something different. In this way, errors of individual perception can blur the distinction between *what's real, what may have happened,* and *what's wishful thinking.* Here's a good example: You're leaving a restaurant after having lunch, and a woman with a large shoulder bag rushes by you in the doorway, knocking you off balance and into a man walking to the door and pulling a cigarette out of a pack. The man drops his cigarette, is peeved that you've banged into him, and mutters a curse at you. The woman who started the domino effect doesn't bother to look back or apologize.

The reality is that this woman behaved rudely, if not witlessly, and unsettled two people—you and the man you fell against. However, she might not be a rude person by habit, and there might have been extenuating circumstances to her rushing out. Maybe she was ill, had just been rejected, was rushing home for an emergency. It does not matter. What matters isn't her story, but your reaction.

Our lives are filled with such irritating little events. But what would your automatic response be? How lingering would the effect of this incident be on you? Would this incident confirm your belief that others shove you around or curse you and don't take a moment to look at how they've hurt you? What if the man you fell against was a Tom Selleck look-alike and attracted you, and you feel wounded that he cursed you instead of asking you for your number? Would the incident become a jumping-off point to feel contempt for all women of the shoulder-bag jostler's type, skin color, or what you perceived as her social station? Or would you gain composure minutes later and soon after, chat casually about the event without feeling you'd been attacked?

⁓

Holding on to little grievances like this for years builds up a distorted sense of reality. It's not that uncommon or far-fetched for this distortion to happen even when the events that caused it are unthreatening or simply part of the pain of growing up. In my practice, I see how women redefine reality to catastrophize noncatastrophic events, create problems where none exist, get lost in illusions or the allure of empty promises. How many women do you know who can tell you about that "one rotten little person" in the third grade, or junior high, or the pushy neighborhood girl who did them wrong in some way? This negative person is as real today as she was yesterday to such a woman, giving her a continuing importance. When you've survived such a person and moved on with your life, you're stronger.

Which brings me back to the question of what's real. Sure, it's true that there's a philosophical difference between "my reality" and "your reality." So is it true that in the world, there are indisputable truths and indisputable realities, such as, the Pacific Ocean is salt water or your eyes are the color they are? How do you know what the truth is when the facts are influenced by emotions or beliefs?

We live in a world of frequently changing partners, fractured relationships, and the specter of fearsome attacks from those who want to see our demise. The world has become unpredictable. As a result, we can lose the ability to be grateful for what we have; instead, we tend to count only what's *missing*. When you accept unpredictability, you appreciate what you have now. What are your expectations?

Every once in a while, it's important to take a tally of the things that are of real and great value in your life and write a couple of sentences that sum them up. This tally includes your love life, your family, your children, your finances, your work, your play, your friends, your health, your sense of self, your ethnicity, and your spirituality.

When you can articulate how you feel, you can plot a trajectory to where you want to be or what you might do to make life better.

Can you roll with life's punches? What's meaningful to you? Asking yourself the important questions will help you sort out your feelings and clarify the direction you need to take to act now. I've provided a list of such questions that follows shortly. Let me suggest a psychological approach as you go through these questions: To get real, you must deal with the answers you first come up with. *Don't edit yourself out*, no matter how shocked you are at your immediate responses. You can edit your answers for anyone else, but do not cheat yourself. If you feel your answer is petty, horrible, or shows you as being lazy or manipulative, don't disown it and say, "That's not me." Instead, accept your response for what it is: the reflection of a facet of your personality that you can learn to deal with, helps others deal with, or have the capability to change. This is your chance to confront your truths. You'll never confront others until you confront yourself.

Here are the questions:

- Do you feel that if something terrible happened to you today, you would have no regrets and feel that your hopes, dreams, goals, and ambitions would be fulfilled?
- Would you describe yourself as being generally optimistic, generally pessimistic, or a little of both, depending on the occasion?
- Do you live your life more to please others than to please yourself?
- Have you allowed any unresolved issues in past bad relationships to stop you from finding love or succeeding at your chosen field?
- Are you willing to take risks, or do you expect others to do for you what you do not do for yourself?
- Do you have a set of personal principles by which you abide, even if others do not agree with you?

- Can you live with disappointment?
- Do you feel as if you are running an obstacle course through stress-filled days? Or do you feel as if you're drifting through life and every day seems the same?
- Are you paralyzed by a fear of not doing things "right"?
- Are you haunted by a sense that life cannot change for you, no matter how much effort you put into the planning?
- Do you have the courage to go back and take care of unfinished business?
- Do you excuse yourself for bad behavior but blame others when things don't go right?
- Can you end a relationship without bitterness and give the other person a chance to adjust to the ending? Do you leave room for people to come back if they want a place in your life?
- Do you accept that others will change and may therefore change their relationship with you, or do you fight to keep things status quo?
- How have you changed in the last six months, or have you changed at all?
- If you could relive your life, would you end up where you are now?
- With whom do you want to spend your time in the next phase of your life? Whom would you spend less time with or drop entirely if you could?
- Without being gloomy, how would your eulogy read now compared with what it could say if you make positive changes in your life?

If you've come up with a few answers that surprised you, that's good. If some questions brought up a sense of failure and negative responses, they are providing you with important information, telling you where you get yourself into trouble or where you are confused. No one grows by believing she is perfect. You either face reality by willingly examining your responses, or you stay the same and continue to not get what you want and have to deal with people walking out on you.

You know who and what is right or wrong for you. If you do things that are not right for you, you've probably wandered from your true self and fallen into relationships by default. Maybe you've put money and acquisitions above all else as the ultimate measure of success. Or perhaps you've handed over the power within your family and community to the kind of men who hold your personal growth in check. Doing this not only perpetuates social tyranny but shows you have a tyrannical definition of reality.

We are all like diamonds in that we are multifaceted. Some people love change and are change masters, while others are reluctant to acknowledge their many facets and therefore fail to shine the way they could. To me, Madonna is one of the few public figures with a canny gift for getting real. That's what so clever about her and probably what accounts for her longevity in the business: she's not only multifaceted, she's a chameleon. Madonna's *ability to stay herself and yet change herself at the same time* is an example to think about. She started out as a dancer, then restyled herself into a provocative, in-your-face wild child wearing thrift-shop chic. Briefly interviewed after her first appearance on television and asked what she wanted to do next, Madonna answered, "I want to rule the world." She said it with a smile, but she wasn't kidding—even if the nation in one voice would have shouted at her, "Get real!" She went on to be a sexual explorer, Hollywood glamour-puss, millionaire business-woman, and now is a bit tamed down and a mother of two.

You may not like her work, but you can actually plot her growth over the years as a performer and a woman. In each phase of being Madonna, she saw life a little differently, and let us know what she would and would not do. Even if she bombed, she shrugged it off and moved forward. She continually recreated herself in order to get the most out of life.

In nature, chameleons adapt to the environment by changing color, blending in, and thus fooling predators. Nothing could be more descriptive of getting real, and rolling with the punches. Although we're a much higher form of life than a chameleon, capable of thinking and having a conscience, we can essentially do the same on another level: adapt to better fit into a personal environment of family, relationships, and work. You may have had twenty jobs in your life, or three failed marriages, and your bombs may be greater than your successes, but if you stretch your ability to adapt to what is real, you can gain the courage to keep going out there and, ultimately, achieve greater success.

If you are in touch with your reality, the moment will come when you feel a change emerging from you. It can come upon you with a start and in a place you don't associate with revelations. For example, you could be in a supermarket checkout line and see the cashier in the next aisle flirting with a customer while she gives him change, and it could come to you: that could be your husband. You've been quarreling a lot lately. He'd be vulnerable to some flirty behavior. Yes, you could stand it if your husband left you after fifteen years of marriage, but, no, you wouldn't like it. You'd feel betrayed and hurt. Yes, you want him to be a part of your life and your children's lives; therefore, you decide to stop pushing him away. You see that you need to accept him as he is, focus on his strengths and stop punishing him for who he isn't. This is clear. It just takes a small turn on your dial of perception and you can feel really good about your life.

In facing reality, recognize that everything wrong with your life isn't because someone else is doing it to you. You're the major participant, not the audience, in your life. If you're sitting around feeling sorry for yourself for what you don't have, think about *what you have*, like your achievements. Appreciate yourself for what you've done so far. While you're at this point, think about *what you don't want, and fortunately, do not have*. Think about everything you can be grateful for.

Whether it's about fulfilling a dream, cutting loose from bad relationships, or pursuing a loving relationship, no matter what your age, begin a plan to get real now. If you want what others have, do the work that would allow you to get those things. Here are a few more questions to ask yourself about getting real:

- How can I improve myself?
- What can I do to make this day better?
- What are the things that didn't go right yesterday that I can use as a map for a new pattern for tomorrow?

Age or circumstances (as long as you're free) should not be a deciding factor to back down from a plan. I recently met an eighty-four-year-old woman who four years previously had left her husband of sixty years for her first boyfriend, Frank. Unhappy for most of her married life, within two weeks of accidentally running into Frank, Estelle had made the decision to spend the remainder of her life with this old love. "I saw Frank and it hit me. I knew I'd made a big mistake having married Joe instead," she said.

She says she's been happier with Frank these last four years than she was the previous sixty with Joe. Being in their eighties, they don't have children to care for and feel they have otherwise met their obligations to others. Neither she nor Frank ever believed "it was too late." Instead, this octogenarian couple saw their union as a real possibility, had the courage to be together for whatever may be the rest of their lives, and took the chance.

Some people think Estelle and Frank are brave and others think they've lost a grip on reality. I take the story for what it is: an unhappy woman found a chance for happiness and took it.

It's not enough to say that things will get better; you have to *make* them better. If you're honest with yourself, if you get real, you will see where you can take action in your own life.

One of the most compelling reasons for personal change is your legacy—to your children, to your community, and to the broader society you live in. By enriching your life, you enrich the lives of those around you and give them hope.

DEFINING WHAT IS IMPORTANT IN LIFE

As I mentioned, you strengthen your real self by clarifying what you think and how you think it. How do *you* figure out which choice to make, which inclination, taste, or option to follow? What follows is a series of ideas that deal with standards, integrity, and choices to help you live in the real world and get more from it.

Making Smart Choices That Keep You Grounded and Away from Excess

The key to making smart choices is in discerning the difference between making a decision and exercising a preference. When you order chocolate over vanilla ice cream, it's a preference, not a decision. Quitting your job to start a home business or marrying for the third time is a decision. The foundation for a better life rests on making decisions in your best interest. It is the ability to make the distinction between what works for today and what makes sense for the rest of your life.

There are moments when temptation—a strong preference—makes the decision for you. But you need to control the temptation for excess. How you conduct yourself sexually and whether you indulge in binge-eating, drugs, alcohol, spending, gambling, or other types of excess has to do with the core of who you see yourself to be. I talk about this with patients who have lost a "center" and seem to live in an emotional centrifuge. They bounce from one bad decision to another bad decision, either seeking sensation to bury reality or playing with sensation to create a reality they can live in. They are on a trampoline, not grounded at all. When you find your center, it will remind you of what your values are and if you're playing with fire.

⁓

The process of making practical decisions involves a few separate thought processes: a sense of responsibility, weighing the possible consequences by balancing risks and benefits, applying experience, and losing the fear of making mistakes. If you *act* as opposed to *react*, you stop making decisions passively and are able to break out of the pattern of continuing bad habits.

When you make the decision to live by just reacting to what comes along next, others call the shots and reality is painful. When you decide to live in excess, impulse will drive you until you're no longer in control—and reality will be even more painful when you come down from the high. The rational consciousness that establishes discipline and makes decisions to ensure your survival is undermined by using a temporarily mind-altering substance. Such temptations call to you, and you need to resist the desire to find satisfaction in them, sometimes at any cost.

You can maintain physical and psychological integrity by deciding to get excess into perspective. The ultimate goal is to help you notch down to a state of moderation or, when possible, elimination of any undesirable activities. Let me ask you some questions here about addictions or binges and when they draw you to them:

- What incidents or feelings trigger the need for such "pleasures"?
- What is pleasurable about the pleasure?
- How does excess truly deplete or energize you?

Another aspect of decision making and getting grounded is to seek out the company of someone who has the kind of wisdom you need to help you change. You're smart to know you need an answer that is outside your knowledge and ability. Thus, there is a place for a "wise person" in your life—a guru, counselor, or mentor, either embodied in one person or many. A person who's wise in the ways that you need wisdom can give you the dose of reality you need. She can also provide enlightenment or serve as a model until you carve out your own signature way of proceeding.

There's an ancient way of wisdom that says, "Emulate the wise man." This tells us to seek and accept a teacher. But how do you choose him? You don't ask a gambler how to invest money or a three-time divorcée how to solve marital problems. My suggestion is to find four "wise women/men" through references or reputation and investigate their credentials and the trust they've built with others. Take the same one key question you need help with to each, and judge for yourself: who gave the best and most doable answer? Weigh their insights and see if they apply to your situation.

Don't take everything a potential adviser says on faith; be discerning and maintain a discriminating mind. Speak to each about contradictions or inconsistencies in their advice and see who is willing to discuss them. If someone demands that anyone who asks his advice must follow and not ask questions, it means he doesn't have the answers, just an inflated ego. You'd be back where you started from if you spent time with this person.

Communicate and Be a Communicator, Part 1: Say What You Mean and Mean What You Say

I heard an interesting story from a friend who runs a small business in L.A. Jackie's secretary had to take a leave of absence because her son became ill and needed her care at home for about a month. Jackie told a friend of hers about her situation, and Bonnie offered to help on a part-time basis for a few days, until the temp arrived. The offer sounded good, especially since Bonnie had once worked for Jackie and pretty much knew what had to be done and how.

Then came the surprise: "Please don't discuss the fact that I'm working here in front of Stan," Bonnie said, referring to her husband. Jackie asked, "Is there a problem with your being here? Please tell me." But Bonnie just said, "Stan doesn't like me helping anyone out, so don't pay me. I would have to account for the money if I deposited your check. I don't want him to know what I'm doing."

It still didn't quite make sense to Jackie. Was Bonnie saying that Stan didn't like Jackie and would resent his wife helping her for that reason? What kind of relationship did Bonnie have with her husband regarding money? Jackie knew that Stan earned over a quarter of a million dollars a year, but that didn't mean they lived within the budget from his income.

Jackie felt caught between needing Bonnie in the office and the unsettling feeling that Bonnie had to lie to Stan to be there. On the last day, Bonnie finally admitted what she could not say at the outset: she doesn't want to work, but Stan thinks she *should* bring a salary to the household. She feared that if Stan found out she was working for Jackie for nothing, he'd pressure her by saying, "If you can work for Jackie for no money, you can work and get paid for it. Get a job." Although Bonnie is pretty honest most of the time, her fear was that Stan would start harping on the theme of her going back to work—a theme she had carefully avoided discussing with him for years.

Bonnie's hedging put Jackie in an awkward spot. Even though Bonnie could not say what she meant and mean what she said, Jackie wanted to compensate Bonnie for her assistance. She resolved the problem by buying Bonnie a gift certificate for a local department store. Stan, they both knew, would be less likely to question her on the appearance of a pair of earrings or a sweater than a company check.

Jackie found a replacement for Bonnie in a few days. She didn't want to be a part of the internal strife of the marriage. She resolved that she would never ask Bonnie to help out again, not because Bonnie wasn't capable, but because Jackie didn't want to be part of a lie.

Communicate by Being a Communicator, Part 2: Listening as Well as Speaking Effectively

"The whole secret of [her] popularity," Milan Kundera says of the character in *The Book of Laughter and Forgetting*, "is that she has no desire to talk about herself. She submits to the forces occupying her ear, never saying, 'it's absolutely the same with me . . .'"

We all understand the opposite of this kind of generosity. Did you ever open a conversation with a friend and have her interrupt you after every phrase, so that it took you a half an hour to tell an anecdote instead of five minutes? You start with, "You won't believe who called me after five years! Remember Dave, the guy who proposed to me and—" Your friend interrupts with, "Don't remind me of old boyfriends. I saw Hal at the mall and he looks like hell. I'm glad I broke up with him . . ." When she takes a breath, you continue with, "But the thing about Dave is that he's getting out of his marriage and—" Your friend breaks in: "I remember a guy who called me in the middle of his divorce and . . ." your friend continues, and so on. Your friend's interruptions make it impossible for you to have any continuity of thought. All her interruptions leave you feeling that she doesn't want to hear about you, she just wants the conversation to be all about her.

Conversation is about communication, and both intimate and social communication require *listening effectively* to be successful. When you listen effectively, you learn the difference between superficial discourse, real opportunities, and demonstrable interest in others. By listening, you learn of another's experiences, appreciations, who they are and what they want—and you find out if they are genuinely friend, foe, or are impartial. The best conversationalist is a good listener. Acting coaches tell actors that listening is one of the most powerful skills they can have.

How do you listen effectively? For one, if you had a long conversation with a business associate, ask yourself how much of the conversation you would remember the next day *in terms of what the associate said.* Is most of your conversation about what you want/your love life/your complaints/your money problems and what the other person can do for you? Do you tend to not only interrupt others, but change the subject back to your interests, or even point out something unremarkable in the surroundings to distract them? Some people do this to simply dominate the conversation and create a sense of self-importance.

Getting real in conversation depends on being able to discuss ideas, events, or feelings without feeling threatened by other points of view. Listening effectively provides you with information that can benefit you as well as forge genuine friendship.

Fulfilling Obligations

"Taking care of business" means protecting yourself in terms of assets, and also getting in touch with the pleasure of fulfilling obligations with integrity. It's not about being a selfless Mother Teresa, but of doing the right thing.

One aspect of fulfilling obligations is taking care of yourself, safeguarding what is yours, and not expecting to be rewarded for recklessness, greed, or feigned stupidity. Gerri is an example of what not to do. When her first marriage ended after seven years, thirty-year-old Gerri settled for $50 a week for child support from a very rich husband who could have afforded more. Her reason: to prove she wasn't mercenary and that she could make it on her sales associate's salary. At age thirty-three, she met Carl, a forty-year-old high-level corporate executive whose relationship with Gerri sealed his decision to get a divorce from his wife. Feeling lucky to be getting married again, Gerri paid no attention to how Carl settled with his-soon-to-be ex-wife.

Shortly before they married, Carl and Gerri bought a house, with Carl promising Gerri he'd put her name on the deed. "I trusted him, and why wouldn't I?" she said. "I was too busy being in love to pay attention to details." He seemed to be glad-handed with money, buying himself and Gerri luxury cars and designer clothes, money obviously being no object. Happy and feeling secure, Gerri quit her job as sales manager at a boutique, and had a child with Carl. Then, one by one, his three children from his first marriage moved in with them. Soon Gerri was housemother to five children, and Carl's three treated her like a hired day worker.

Carl began a lucrative sideline as a consultant, but she never saw any of the high fees. Carl, she'd soon find out, had begun gambling heavily and paying for the lavish lifestyle of a girlfriend across town. After ten years of marriage, Gerri filed for divorce.

"Everything I didn't pay attention to came back to haunt me," she said, a year into court battles with her husband. "For one, ask how I felt when I discovered Carl owned the house outright? He'd never put my name on the deed. I couldn't get any of his tax statements because I never signed one. Our cars were leased, and Carl's business property was heavily mortgaged. Worse, he'd taken out two huge loans on his pension account and cut me out as beneficiary. So while my husband was living like a rich exec, it was all debt. In fact, he didn't provide me with any benefits."

Reality was strong medicine for Gerri. She took a few refresher business courses and went back to sales. While she's still living in the home she thought she co-owned, she can't afford repairs on it, nor will Carl pay for them. In her late forties now, Gerri regrets that she didn't take a more active role in her life with Carl. She never protected herself, never foreseeing how she was putting herself and her child in financial jeopardy. She now believes that marriage is no different from running a business in that you have to be a partner in everything that matters.

If you don't take care of yourself, don't expect others to do it for you.

One of the tendencies many women have, and it's not our finest characteristic, is to turn against ourselves. Women are typically introspective and self-blaming. All the research has shown that men blame others and women blame themselves. That's a fact, an ancient one, that began when Adam in the Garden of Eden disobeyed God and took a bite of the apple. God asked something like, "Why did you disobey me?" and Adam said, pointing to Eve, "she made me do it." This is one of the first cases of discharging personal responsibility.

Like Gerri, women are willing to say, "It's my fault," but it's harder for them to say, as Adam could not, "I take responsibility for my life." This is probably the most important statement you can make. No one else is responsible for you or for fulfilling your obligations to yourself. You have to walk away from the spongers, the whiners, and the desperate ones, including walking away from yourself if this describes you. That is, if you want a different life, you must, above all, *change*.

Gerri's story give us another lesson in *miscommunication*. Here were two people living in the same house for a decade, but they did not understand each other or have a *consensus of definition*. Gerri's definition of marriage was having a man, a house, a child, and appearing normal and right to the world. Carl's definition of marriage was doing what he wanted and spending recklessly without having to account for it. Gerri put herself in Carl's hands because she did not want to take care of herself by checking if he was telling her the truth. She preferred to live passively, depending on him to "do the right thing." He effectively stole from her and used her to raise his children.

Gerri would have fared better had she defined marriage as a real partnership, one in which she had an active role and where there was a checks-and-balances system. To her, marriage is a deep and affectionate relationship with a man who wants to share his life and his worldly goods. She needed to know whether Carl agreed with this definition. She allowed Carl's violations of her beliefs to pile up for years. She saw, but didn't want to focus on, what was really going on because then she would have to take action. That was more work then she wanted. So she just hoped for the best, and lost. Arguing from hindsight is never going to get you any consensus.

The most important consensus of definitions in your life are those between you and your *chosen* significant other. It's different with your parents. When you're grown up, you can accept or reject what your parents believe without it necessarily influencing your daily life. That is not the case with your life's partner. This is why really knowing who you are marrying is so important. This is the person who *will* influence your daily life.

There's no question that if you communicate at a true level of understanding where both of you speak the same language—which very few couples do—your marriage will stand on a unified and intimate foundation. We know that Gerri and Carl miscommunicated what they wanted from marriage.

But what about the consensus of definition in phrases like, "I love you?" When I ask patients the meaning of that phrase, they often answer: "Isn't that obvious? Love is about deep affection, attraction, and possible commitment." Maybe not!

A man says to you, "I love you," and you wonder, "Does he mean he wants what's best for me, or what's best for him?" And, "Does he mean he's willing to put me in the center of his life on occasion, or does he mean that I will always be at the center of his life?" Then again, does his "I love you" mean, "Now you are my possession, and I'll love you as long as you're my wife and do as I ask"? Will he love you if you are your own person and sometimes disagree with him?

There is an old story that a man says "I love you" to get sex and a woman gives sex to hear "I love you." Of course, this isn't true all the time, nor true of people who meant it when they said "I love you" fifteen years ago. In that case, the question to ask is, "When did you stop loving me?"

A conversation that might bring real intimacy of communication to couples would begin with the question, "What does 'I love you' mean to you?" It could mean you care about the man's needs and feelings. It could mean that you want him in your life but don't want him to commandeer it in any way. It could mean his opinion is important to you as long as the two of you make the major decisions and he writes the checks on time.

The more you leave unsaid, whether about the meaning of love that you feel you are being taken for granted, the greater the chance that there will come a defining moment in the relationship. Perhaps it will be an explosive one—when all those unspoken thoughts will come pouring out. The guy will get up from the table and knock over a glass of wine, and all your suppressed thoughts about the relationship will soak up the mess. You'll be angry and possibly make a comment like, "There you go again, giving me extra work." Your boyfriend/spouse responds with, "What's with you? It was an accident." The exchange escalates into an argument.

Arguments can both conceal and reveal real feelings. Instead of going on the offensive over spilled wine, you need to get real and tell the truth. It could be a line like, "I've been holding on to an issue for a long time and have to talk about it. I'm sorry I didn't tell you sooner." Hopefully, he will answer with, "I'm glad you're telling me how you feel. And I'm sorry you didn't tell me about it five years ago when it first came up."

If you are uncertain about speaking up because you fear what the other person will say, here I can state that *uncertainty offers promise*. When you go into a relationship, there's always as much room for surprise as there is for certainty. People are not always predictable, and they can be moved by your being candid and honest. This confrontation of the most communicative type can be a great opportunity for a learning experience. If you know how everything will turn out all the time, what do you have? Not progress.

If you're a couple who cares about each other, analyze your arguments. Decide if you're still acting out versions of the same fight you had years ago, or if what you're arguing about is dead on the truth or circling it. Research shows that most fights are about control and responsibility, or intimacy and distance. We feel them as fights for survival: who will have control, and whether being close means too close to breathe. Examine your quarrels and you will find that they are often another version of the same fight yet again because the underlying issues have never been resolved.

Maintain a Sense of Humor

Keeping a sense of humor makes life's travails easier on the system. I have great faith in the human ability to make the best of what doesn't work out. One of the easier ways to cope with disappointment is through humor. It moderates the hurts of failure, brings you squarely into the moment, and even lets you joke about what you may have felt like crying about.

Humor not only lightens the load, but also gives you a wider perspective on what you're doing and why. A joke can contain insight, and it usually contains some kernel of truth. Humor helps in relationships by defusing uncomfortable or embarrassing moments, and it often draws people to you.

Taking Risks—Getting on to the Stage of Your Own Life

I know a woman who is professional, athletic, and generally optimistic, but she also has many fears and a lot of paranoia about getting on a plane. Polly wants to snorkel in southern Mexico, see the

Great Barrier Reef in Australia, and run a 10K race in Ireland and visit her grandmother, still living there in the countryside. But Polly is so afraid to fly that she never takes a vacation unless she can drive or be driven to the location.

Polly thought about how she's been able to take risks in work, really get out there and compete, and she gave herself a talking-to about flying: she was missing out on too many events and travel experiences, and life was short. Finally, she booked a flight with her running pals, all of whom she knows casually but trusts. She has defeated many of her monsters to get on a plane, with the support of friends. She did it for the pure joy of making a trip and running in a different country. Polly is thrilled that she got herself together. It made a huge difference in her life.

Another approach to breaking through the fear of taking risks is by literally getting on stage. New Yorker Linda Amiel Burns runs a six-week course called "The Singing Experience" that helps you tap into the connection between singing in public and gaining self-assurance. For the workshop finale, Linda books a small nightclub where for one night all her students get to perform. Linda has coached people of every age and from every walk of life, including, among others, actor Danny Aiello and Bill Geist, a reporter on CBS's *Sunday Morning*. One of her devoted followers has taken eighty workshops.

The workshop premise is elegant: by singing, you learn to suspend self-consciousness, work through emotional barriers that keep tripping you up, and command attention from others. Also, by performing in front of other people, you learn to accept applause and hear it as appreciation or love and *believe you deserve it*. As Linda says, "You learn to applaud yourself."

The process goes a lot deeper than just having fun with a karaoke setup and microphone. "It's not about being a great singer or being a contender on *American Idol*," says Linda. "The workshop is totally noncompetitive; it's about communicating the best of who you are. People come to me emotionally wounded from one thing or another. Some people are angry or shy or fearful, and others are still traumatized from 9/11."

Over the years, Linda developed her risk- and confidence-building techniques to break down barriers. She has what she calls her "magic bag," into which every student is asked to put their "two top" excuses or reasons for not doing what they want to do: "I'm afraid to fail," "my mother-in-law lives with us," "I'm too thin/too old/too fat," and so on. Then she tackles fear, deconstructing it into non-fearful components. "When you're frightened, whether it's at a job interview, or because some woman at a workshop wants you to sing, focus in on your physical responses," she explains. "Maybe it's, 'I'm making a fool of myself . . . my palms are getting sweaty . . . I stutter.' I say, okay, *greet* the response. Take away its power by saying, 'Hello, sweaty palms; hello, bad stutter,' and keep at it. Deal with each fearful response as it comes up."

Twenty-five years of experience has shown Linda that a fear of risk-taking is usually linked to a message parents may have given us as kids. "We're not supposed to *shine*," she said. "It's considered vain or exhibitionistic. But using art to express emotion helps release the negative holds over you. When you sing, there's a combination of floating in the music, with people supporting you, of making the lyrics mean something to you. Singing always changes you, even fractionally. It gives you a sense of confidence you can summon when you need it, on so many levels."

Linda's work has impacted personally, too. A few years ago, right before a workshop performance, Linda got a call that her son had been in a car accident and was in a coma in an Oregon hospital. Utterly distressed, she arrived at the club, told her students about Jason, and explained that she might not function well that night.

"They surrounded me with love and support and made a group prayer for my son's recovery," she said.

"That's when the magic of the stage kicked in and gave me some relief. For those few hours, all was right with the world. I could get myself together for the challenges ahead. I kept sending messages to Jason in my head during the whole show: 'Hang on; Mom's on her way.' "

Linda took a late flight out and got to the hospital's trauma unit the next morning. Jason looked in bad shape. Linda held his hand, felt a squeeze, and was told by the nurses that it was merely a spasm. Then he opened his eyes and muttered, "Hi, Mom." He eventually recovered completely.

Singing from the heart is clearly one way for some people to get real.

Resist Social Pressures That Undermine Your Individuality

Anne Frank, the twelve-year old girl who kept a diary while confined to an attic during the Nazi occupation of Holland wrote, "Nobody need wait a moment longer before starting to improve the world."

It's possible to manage social pressures and stay within the boundaries of good sense and personal scruples. When you're real, you

- Don't lower the bar of acceptable social behavior.
- Know what is right for you and don't look to others to lead you into trends or choices that will ultimately hurt you.
- Don't look to people to give you honor. Seeking recognition for the sake of notoriety or boastful pride can backfire.
- Don't live for others or base your lifestyle on what gives you status in the eyes of others.
- Do resist the temptation to walk down a path with the wrong companions, no matter how glamorous they are.

FINALLY . . .

When you get real, you find humility and can check the position of "the bar" in your own life. I've asked you to answer many questions in this chapter, but please ask yourself a few more. Your answers to the following questions can help you further clarify your thinking right now:

- How do you view your life?
- Are you the one in charge of most of the decisions you make about yourself?
- Do you feel that you are only using a small part of your talent and energy?
- Are you still obsessing about the past, robbing yourself of the ability to stay focused on the present?
- What's really stopping you from moving ahead with your life? Are you being honest with yourself about why you're delaying action?
- What important decisions are you putting off?
- What do you value that's already a part of your life?
- Do you compromise your standards out of expediency, going along to get along? Do you lower the bar of acceptable standards of behavior just to prove something to others?
- Do you find yourself feeling put upon by small daily events?
- Do you make unimportant remarks or events into catastrophes? If so, what's the payoff?
- Do you edit reality so that you don't have to face the truth?
- Do you know the difference between need and want?
- Do you make practical decisions, or do you live in excess?
- Do you mean what you say and say what you mean?

8

EMOTIONAL FULFILLMENT

Happiness Is What You're Willing to Accept

My friend Gloria eventually got colitis she believes, as a result of too many years of forcing herself to smile in the presence of others. Her mother raised her to believe that the road to acceptance and popularity for a girl was to "be nice and look happy." The subtext was clear enough: if she appeared to be happy, she'd attract good things, good men, and guarantee herself a happy life.

Gloria smiled all through her girlhood, her teenage years, through her first marriage, and, even though she was in pain, she was as nice as possible during her divorce. By then, she was so "happy," she was on medication for colitis.

"I played being the good girl," she said. "I just couldn't do enough for you. I didn't even know what the word anger meant. I never felt it. *Really*. If you did things to upset me, I'd tell myself it was *me*, and ignore that I didn't feel good about what was going on. I always made excuses for my husband's behavior and asked people to be understanding. I don't know how anyone could stand being around me."

Gloria speaks about herself differently now. She's at a point where, finally, she knows everyone doesn't have to like her, and she can speak openly about how she feels. "To tell the truth," she added, "I have to check myself and calm down. It's liberating to tell it as it is, and I'm afraid I sometimes overdo it. But I'm so much happier, and now when I smile it's for real."

We're socialized to smile, or else we're considered aloof, unfriendly, unapproachable, or elitist. I'd have loved the opportunity to talk to Gloria's mother and help her understand that smiling and happiness are not necessarily the same. Let's consider the sociology of smiling: one of the first ways people learn to deflect possible attack is by looking nonthreatening and pleasant, hence nature provided us with the ability to smile. A smile says, "I'm safe," and, by further suggestion, "I like you," or "I like what's going on around me," whether or not it's true.

My friend Gloria was raised to smile and project happiness to the world, but pictures of her back then reveal a telltale sign that her world was not peaches and cream: hers was an insincere smile that did not engage her entire face. Gloria smiled, but not always from the heart. You can look at photos of yourself, your family, your friends, and see who's smiling a *real* smile—where the corners of the mouth turn up, *and* the skin at the outer corners of the eyes wrinkle toward the temple.

Who was really happy when the picture was snapped? Studies have correlated the incidence of sincere smiles in photos to later satisfaction in life. That is, you can actually predict whether or not the person smiling will be happy by checking out the whole face. Studies on the subject, says Martin Seligman in his book *Authentic Happiness,* conclude that a sincere, or "Duchenne" smile indicates that you're more likely to get and stay married and experience life-long personal well-being. A mere crinkling of the eyes can tell you something important about yourself. And so will your actions.

THE ANATOMY OF HAPPINESS

I have a colleague who says, "For a baby, happiness is the default position." He's right. Babies don't know about unhappiness, dissatisfaction, or failure. They can experience physical discomfort and fear, but unless they are ill or neglected, they're happy most of the time because their souls operate from a feeling of trust. This feeling of trust remains the ultimate key to happiness. If you're happy with what you have and who you are, you experience more happiness in your life. If you're unhappy with what you have or who you are, you still have an opportunity to change that situation and ultimately find satisfaction.

What is happiness all about? To answer that question, first, as with love, you require *a definition* of what happiness means to you. Your definition must include two key ingredients for happiness to be lasting: (1) *the ability to experience positive emotions and* (2) *to be optimistic*. Let's discuss these ideas one at a time.

Defining Happiness

There are a lot of buzz words that people use without thinking of the real meaning, and "happiness" is one of them. Happiness is more than the momentary feeling that life is good, that you've been lucky, or that you're on top of the world. Happiness always has complexity and changeability, an engagement of the senses and sensibility. It's always a fascinating subject—something everyone wants and too few of us actually achieve. What makes people happy?

- "I pick six numbers and win the lottery, and boy would I be happy."
- "Happiness is finding someone who 'gets you,' likes being with you, and knows how to fix stuff around the house."
- "Happiness is a screen test, a movie deal, and fame."
- "The only thing that would make me happy is a rich man."
- "Who could be happy without love?"
- "Happiness is my husband not fighting with my parents every time they're in the same room."

- "Happiness is making a difference in other people's lives and knowing you're leaving something good behind you when you die."
- "Happiness is eating chocolate all day, staying skinny enough to wear designer clothes, hiring Ray Charles to sing at my wedding, and owning a huge house on Lake Michigan."

Interestingly, some of these definitions are about *momentary pleasures*, *immediate highs*, goals, or achievements, not lasting happiness. Happiness is a means, not an end. It's not a final goal, but an ongoing aspiration, with no finality. That is, you cannot outline a course of action and strive to achieve it, like building a business or finding a life partner. What you *can* achieve is a sense of happiness by having built a business that's successful, or having helped create the right relationship. Happiness doesn't stop when you attain a goal so you could say, "Okay—I'm here at last with my fill of happiness," then stop feeling happy. Rather, you continue to create your own ongoing happiness. And like life itself, happiness and how you define it will change as life changes you.

Where is this elusive thing called happiness found? It's not only at your fingertips—*your happiness comes from within*.

Winning the lottery, ending the habit of fighting with your in-laws, or being able to eat high-sugar/high-fat food without gaining weight would be shortcuts to feeling good only in a fantasyland. This phenomenon is something very different from happiness. The school of thought called positive psychology helps explain it. Positive psychology focuses on the meaning of happy and unhappy moments and says that it's not just that we seek out positive feelings, but that we also want to feel entitled to them. There are many truncated routes to simply feeling good temporarily: drugs, sugar, casual sex, masturbation, marathon shopping, addiction to television, or eating supersize meals. Any of these activities, if they are your cup of tea, can make you feel better for the moment. And you may even feel you deserve the indulgence to relieve yourself of the stress or the misery of the day. But you won't gain lasting happiness this way.

Wealth may bring more possessions but it has surprisingly low correlations with your level of happiness. Loss or lowering of income, both of which have risen dramatically in America despite it being a prosperous nation, do not really affect the level of satisfaction in life. And even though the number of women who undergo plastic surgery has risen a hundredfold in the last ten years, physical attractiveness doesn't have much effect on happiness, either. You can indulge yourself in all the wonderful goodies money can buy and still be starving spiritually. Momentary happiness is not all that filling. A brick of chocolate or a pair of designer shoes will not bring you to the gates of happiness.

Since we're human and fallible, we also have a capacity to readily adapt to good things and soon take them for granted. So in less than three months, a life-changing event such as being promoted, coming into money, or being married can lose its impact on our happiness level. The pleasant life may be had by driving a Porsche, but not the good life, which produces authentic happiness.

Why do you seek happiness in these temporal things as you do? Were you raised to believe that food or sugar or alcohol assuages neglect, punishment, fear, doubt, lack of confidence, and lack of motivation? Can you blame it on your DNA? I'm a psychologist who believes that we are all responsible for how we behave, yet I cannot ignore some of the research that claims that roughly 50 percent of almost every personality trait is attributable to genetic inheritance.

That roughly 50 percent may account for a predisposition to a temperament that tends toward a high level or low level of optimism, meaning a general sense of happiness and well-being. If yours is on a low level, you'll need to summon all your fortitude and determination to work against depression and pessimism.

My professional "mentor," Martin Seligman, Ph.D., whose book *Authentic Happiness* is a seminal work on the subject, studies every aspect of happiness—from how it appears to how it really operates, both physically and psychologically. Of the many works I've investigated on the subject, Dr. Seligman's theories make the most sense to me and are similar to my own ideas.

True happiness is about feeling good from having exercised your signature strengths and virtues, not by tallying your external assets. Signature strengths are deeply characteristic for each of us, and each time we use them we feel good about ourselves. The greatest success and the deepest emotional satisfaction arise from building and using these strengths. These are qualities like kindness, curiosity, loyalty, and spirituality. They allow us to take the focus off ourselves and feel a part of something larger. Perseverance, perspective, fairness, and courage are other strengths, but they are called upon when you are challenged; therefore, we may not be able to be in touch with them on a daily basis.

Happiness and well-being are anchored to greater entities—your signature strengths and how they affect the meaning of your life. I find that some women don't admit to being happy, believing that the meaning of life is to live with limits or deprivation. They have a superstitious belief that if they acknowledge happiness, it will be snatched from them. Other women believe that the meaning of life is about suffering, and that happiness suggests a shallow personality with weak moral grounding.

As with love, you help yourself get what you want by defining happiness for yourself. Be honest with yourself. Is happiness for you about what you gain, rather than what you give, or what you have *more of* as compared with what others have less of? Is happiness a matter of inner peace, good relationships, contentment with your work, and a quiet life? Is happiness connected with being left alone to do your work? Is it connecting at the most profound level with creativity, whether it is gardening, teaching children to ice-skate, writing poetry, or baking cookies? Is happiness a matter of faith, or a deep spirituality?

Emotional Fulfillment

Let me pose a few questions to start you off. Look back and ask yourself,

- When in your life did you feel satisfied or happy?
- What was going on—did it connect with a love relationship, a job, having a child, working on a hobby like painting, singing in a chorus, or rebuilding the kitchen cabinets?
- Did you win an award? What was it for, and do you still have those qualities that got you such an acknowledgment? Was the award about doing good for others, doing good work, or for looking good?

Where is your happiness found? An old adage says that if you don't know where you're going, any road will take you there. When you stop wandering and know where you're going, you can find a route to take you there.

What if you get there and it doesn't make you happy? A patient told me she wanted a divorce after fifteen bitter years of marriage, that she believed freedom from her husband, Don, would save her life and make her happy. She fully believed this. Don was overbearing and seemed to treat her badly so he could feel better about himself. All Sally talked about was the bliss of life without Don. When her husband suddenly left her, she was so stricken with pain she could not even sit on a chair to talk about it—she sobbed on the floor.

I suggested to Sally that in a year she'd thank him for leaving. Within a year and a half, Sally figured out that she didn't have to surrender her life ever again to a man who'd keep her down to fulfill his needs. Her own definition of happiness was no longer marriage at any cost but was about self-respect and moving out of the way of bullies. Two years later, Sally met a man through her job who really loved her, something she'd never believed possible. Now she thanks Don for giving her another chance by leaving her.

It can happen this way, too. Sue, a beautiful woman of forty-five, came to see me after being physically abused by her husband. She'd married Ben shortly after her first husband died. At that time she was thirty-five years old with three children to raise on her own. She couldn't imagine going on alone, so when Ben, her late husband's buddy, asked her out, she was happy to go.

Within a year, they married. Ben was five years her junior, and Sue felt lucky, in fact, *grateful* that a young single man would be willing to take on a whole family. One by one, her children moved out to live with their uncles, finding Ben's verbal and emotional abuse intolerable. Sue defended him, making excuses for him like, "His back hurts . . . his boss pushes him around . . . his best friend died . . . his mother calls and nags." A year ago, her oldest daughter was visiting and asked her why she was wearing sunglasses in the house. "Ran into a door," Sue told her.

After ten years of marriage, Sue missed having her children with her and only had Ben to come home to. She worked long hours at her job to compensate for the loss of income—Ben was now on disability for his bad back. She'd come home, cook his dinner, and then have to hear him rant about her poor housekeeping. Then there was the physical abuse. Sue was desperately unhappy and finally left him.

The first time I saw her in my office, she was scared. "I've never lived on my own and I don't know if I can. I've never been so unhappy. Help me," she said. In response, I told her, "Whatever you do, don't speak to Ben or see him for at least three months. If you feel that you must maintain a connection, promise yourself that if you still want to talk to him then, we'll discuss it."

I saw Sue twice a week for two weeks, then once a week, then every two weeks. We just celebrated her two-month anniversary of living on her own. She loves it! She's made new friends, signed up for courses in Japanese and drama, and lives on her own schedule. Her wardrobe has changed from gray and black to bright colors.

"I'm so happy," she said. "For the first time in years, I've become my own person. I like myself. I was so weak before, I can't believe it was me. Never again will I hand myself over to someone else. I've found such strength in going through this. This is how I always wanted to be."

If there's a lesson in these stories, it's that you can't make one road the only one to happiness, whether it's personal or career-related. The important thing is to define where you want to go. Sally and Sue thought marriage defined their happiness, but marriage involved men who were destroyers of happiness. They both had to honestly examine what fulfillment really meant, so they would not only seek it, but know it when they got it.

Both women had another belief: that no matter how painful life was, it would improve. It was an inner sense of optimism that made them believe they could put one foot in front of the other and make the effort. But, like these women, you have to point your feet in a positive direction.

In truth, happiness rarely springs from limitations or suffering. But it does arise from the exercise of strength and virtue through *positive emotion and positive action.*

Positive Emotions

The afterglow of easy pleasurable activity, like hanging out with friends or eating ice cream out of its container, pales in comparison to the effects of positive action motivated by positive emotions. In this state, you are kind and giving to others. Kindness consists of total engagement with someone else's needs and a loss of self-consciousness. Mother Teresa's legendary kindness could allow her to suspend her fear of death and disease and pick up nearly dead people off the Calcutta streets. We may not be like Mother Teresa, but there are daily acts of kindness that we can do. The result is a sense of well-being that comes from using your strengths and virtues. You know that you are making use of the best part of you. Those actions imbue your life with authenticity and foster that elusive feeling called happiness.

We may be sensate beings, but feelings are momentary occurrences, expressed in response to a circumstance. As you watch a documentary on the Civil War, a voice-over reading of a letter from a dead soldier makes you cry. You see footage of a war somewhere in the world on the news, and it makes you angry or repulsed by violence. So your feelings can change; they need not be a reoccurring and fixed feature of your personality. However, it is different with *positive emotion and the need to express it*. When positive emotion is distanced from your personality, you go through life feeling empty or depressed. You become cynical, even bitter. You may view your life as just marking time. Being future-oriented allows you to be hopeful, so that even when you are experiencing a bad time, you realize it will not last the rest of your life.

THE CONNECTION BETWEEN HAPPINESS AND OPTIMISM

Optimism and hope have great power to change your thinking and thus, your mood. These qualities are great aids in rallying when bad events strike and can even help you fight disease. The concepts of happiness and optimism have been extensively researched. Let's look at *optimism* and why it affects what you get out of life. Then we'll examine *pessimism*, and you decide which gives you the greater chance at happiness.

Current research suggests that there's a big difference between how optimists and pessimists regard failure. Optimists regard failure as a result of a decision they made themselves. A relationship falls apart, and the optimist says, "I made a mistake. I can learn from this and not repeat it again." Pessimists, however, attribute failure to *a part* of themselves they believe they cannot change, such as, "I'm not smart enough/pretty enough/privileged enough," etc. Their view is that it will never get better. Pessimists also tend to be blamers and lack trust in others.

Optimists can evaluate what they've done realistically. They can appraise their abilities and the extent of the "x" factor of luck and say, "I'm talented and I do good work. I can depend on myself." A pessimist having a triumph would point to a transient cause, such as, "It was my lucky day," or, "The other woman didn't show up, so I got the job." Optimists can put their troubles in a box and go on with their lives while pessimists keep picking at old problems or allow one big problem to bleed all over the others. An optimist can use a little makeup to mask a pimple on her face and go on with her day. A pessimist is sure that everyone is staring at her blemish and she can't think of anything else.

So while optimists tend to interpret problems or setbacks as short-term, controllable, and specific, pessimists see their troubles as long-term, as potentially undermining other plans, and as uncontrollable. It is no surprise to learn that optimists outlive pessimists by a 19 percent longer life span. Pessimists are eight times more likely to become depressed, have worse physical health, and rockier interpersonal relationships.

Optimists do not catastrophize unless they are in a real catastrophe, and they are quicker to get a grip on reason. Pessimists tend to catastrophize across the board; therefore, when one thread of their life weakens or breaks, the whole fabric unravels. They're not disappointed—they're devastated. They don't have stomach pain—they're sure it's an ulcer. They're not short of cash—they're near bankruptcy. They didn't just lose a job—they are losers.

Pessimists complain about a global unfairness—as if everyone everywhere had no sense of justice—instead of singling out the one person who might be unfair to them. As pain and disappointment are parts of life, so is rejection. Think of a guy cruising for a woman in a singles' bar. It's his goal to go home with a woman. He may approach ten women and the first nine turn him down. Fortunately for him, he's not out of the game, because the tenth woman says yes. If he's a pessimist, he'll think, "Oh, great, right . . . striking out again! I'm getting crushed here," after the second rejection, and become more and more bitter in his approach, guaranteeing turndowns, including one from that tenth woman.

Disappointment about work can sometimes feel worse than pain about love, because work is about survival. Rejection, unfortunately, is part of the pursuit. One of my patients just lost her job, and with a fifteen-year-old daughter to support, she's scared she won't find any good job prospects. Brenda sent out résumés, and so far, she received four rejections, but she's also set up two appointments.

When she called me to give a progress report, I could tell she was dejected. Brenda's voice gave her away. She sounded angry and annoyed at the position she found herself in. "This is going to be a disaster," she said. "There's going to be too much driving to get to one job . . . the woman who's interviewing me for the second job sounded so superior, like she was doing me a favor . . . I'm not sure what to wear and if I can get into my gray suit . . . I'll never forgive my ex-husband for running out on me and getting away with murder on the child support . . ."

It was clear to me that if Brenda went to her interviews loaded down with woes and acting as if she had no hope of being hired, her prophecy would be fulfilled. She was speaking as though she was daring someone to hire her.

Pessimists like Brenda do not depersonalize rejection and move on easily. If she were more optimistic, she'd take serial rejection as what she has to endure to get what she wants. Then she could leave disappointments behind her, not add them on to the pile of woes and take them with her to the next interview.

Optimism doesn't exist in a dreamy, blissful, ninny state in which you believe things will work out without making an effort. Optimism is not entitlement. You can *learn* optimism and reap its rewards. Thus, *learned optimism*, as Dr. Seligman calls it, is a way to eradicate pessimism.

There's a difference between *positive thinking* and *learned optimism*. The process of positive thinking usually involves the repetition of upbeat statements or "affirmations," such as the classic, "Every day in every way I'm getting better and better," or, "I am worthy." You can repeat these affirmations from sunup to sunset, but unless you do something to prove to yourself that you're actually improving, they are just words. In learned optimism, you search for evidence that punches holes in your catastrophic explanations or distorted thinking. Mastering learned optimism is truly one of the blessings of growing up. Life works when you have reality on your side and the skills to recognize it.

How can you break out of pessimistic patterns and learn to be an optimist? The psychological energy generated by optimism and hope is capable of causing a real physical transformation. Belief that everything will be all right can strengthen resistance to depression and disease. Psychologist Albert Ellis studied this phenomenon and found it true. Seligman observed that if you think about bad events in terms of *always* rather than as transitional, you end up having a pessimistic style.

Pessimism keeps you in the past and spinning your wheels. But the habit of thinking pessimistically can be broken by following these three steps:

1. Intellectually let go of any ideology that says your past will determine your future.
2. Review your memories, then focus on, and voluntarily increase, your gratitude for the good things you have, and forgive past wrongs.
3. Have positive emotions about the future. Those emotions center on faith, trust, confidence, and hope.

How do you accomplish these steps? First identify your negative thoughts and treat them *as though they were uttered by a rival* whose mission in life is to make you miserable. Would you take the word of a rival who wants domain over your thinking process? Probably not. By disconnecting your pessimistic thoughts from your personality, you're more able to fight them. For example, if you find yourself thinking, "Everyone is unfair," pretend your "rival" is telling you that. Now check out the accuracy of the charge. Ask yourself

- What evidence is there for this belief? What makes you believe "people" are unfair?
- What's gone bad? Why?
- What do you want people to give you? And how many people have extended themselves and been more than fair to you?

You might also ask yourself these questions to reveal something important about your thinking:

- What good would it do for you to dwell on the belief that the world *should* be fair?
- Would life be better, and ultimately, more "fair," if you changed the situation so that it does not happen again in the future?

Another good exercise to fight pessimism is to practice facing what you think are adverse situations in your daily life and tune in closely to the beliefs you repeat to yourself. For some women, adversity takes the shape of minor events, such as the repairman being hours late or a friend you haven't seen in a few weeks still not returning your call. List the consequences of what occurs because of the pessimistic beliefs that leave you feeling unsatisfied or feeling overlooked or treated inequitably. Learn to dispute these beliefs vigorously.

When you figure out your thinking processes, you not only find the truth, you sharpen your reflexes about your beliefs and you learn optimism.

Now, how do you think about your past? In Chapter 2 I spoke about the connection between past events and your growing up. In this chapter I want to help you look at past events with another perspective: ridding yourself of any ideology that says your past must determine whether you feel happy in your adult life.

All the emotions you feel about your past are subject to interpretation. This one idea can be the key to understanding your past in the proper context. If you believe that what happened long ago still determines what will happen in the future, then you're right. Events will follow the course you believe they are destined to follow. If you're told, or you tell yourself, that wanting to better your life is reaching too far, you'll end up passively giving in to circumstances.

A friend of mine who grew up in a Bronx tenement was determined to have a better life than the bleak one of her neighborhood, even though her parents believed that she'd be slapped down for wanting more. Simone eventually achieved her goal. When she was in her late forties, she did volunteer work coaching dropouts for their high school diplomas. It turned out that one of the students, a twenty-two-year-old man who worked as a messenger on Wall

Street, still lived blocks from where Simone grew up. The young man was shocked that they'd both gone to the same public and junior high schools. He said to her, "If you're from the 'hood, how come you sound like *Lifestyles of the Rich and Famous*? Simone knew exactly why he had initially thought that she'd had an easier, more privileged life than he. She answered, "I'm living proof that you can leave the old neighborhood and do what you want." Determined optimism had led her out.

It would have been simple for Simone to take the path of least resistance and surrender to the ethos of the neighborhood: other people succeed, not underdogs like us. Simone wouldn't surrender her life to a place she did not like and take up permanent residence there just because her parents had. She wasn't a blamer, for one, and she could see only misery in her future, not happiness, by staying there.

Newer studies in psychology are examining the veracity of blaming adult depression, anxiety, bad marriages, drug use and abuse, sexual problems, serial unemployment, aggression against your children, alcoholism, and anger that's acted out on others on what happened to you as a child. The major traumas of your childhood have some influence on your personality as an adult, but only a *barely detectible* one.

You choose how to think about yourself. Many people are unduly embittered about their past and therefore passive about their future because they believe personal history has imprisoned them. This is an attitude that fuels a psychological infrastructure that drives you into victimology. The only result of victimology is that it overrides the sense of individual responsibility and the impulse for rugged individualism that used to be this nation's hallmark.

Take this opportunity to review your memories. Focus on, and voluntarily increase, your gratitude for the good things you have, and forgive past wrongs. You cannot do anything to change the past. If you think it has offered you very little, bid it good-bye. Why hold on to something that continues to hurt you? If it offered you a lot and you have less now, figure out how to even things out so that you feel content, or make peace with less. There are many good reasons to make peace with and free yourself from your past: less depression, less anger, more living in the present, and more having enthusiasm for the future.

My third suggestion is to adopt positive emotions about the future. These would center on faith, trust, confidence, and hope. Positive emotions do not include anger, revenge, or cruelty. This is an angry world we live in, with anger within your own four walls as likely as anger on the streets, anger in entertainment, and anger on an international scale.

Anger has explosive and dangerous qualities, and if dwelling on the past makes you angry, and you keep expressing it, you'll feel the blast one way or another. Expressing anger is one factor responsible for increasing the incidence of cardiac disease. Researchers have found that Type A personalities, who tend to be driven by ambition, do not suffer by suppressing anger but rather by showing it openly. In one study, 255 medical students took a personality test that measured overt hostility. Researchers went back and looked at them twenty-five years later. The angriest people had roughly five times as much heart disease as the least angry.

It doesn't sound possible, but squelching and controlling rage makes your blood pressure go down. Expressing hostile emotions or even mentally dwelling upon them will raise blood pressure. Biology thus makes this point: if you stay angry about past wrongs that you cannot change, you get caught in a vicious cycle that tosses you around, psychologically and physically.

A patient once said to me, "Isn't it easier to just forget and start over?" It *is* easier, but there are no known ways to enhance the process of forgetting and to voluntarily suppress memories. In fact, attempts to suppress thoughts will backfire on you. It is like being told, "Do not think about a brown bear walking toward you," and, of course, the image is fixed in your consciousness. It is your job to undo the destructive habit of getting trapped in an angry past by being flexible, creative, and generating alternatives. Thus, you *replace* the picture of the brown bear with a picture of a butterfly or something else. And you replace negative thoughts with positive ones rather than just trying to erase the negative ones.

This is a good argument for you to appreciate and savor the good moments in your past and to stop overemphasizing the bad ones or giving them an importance that is way out of proportion. An appreciation for what went right bolsters serenity, contentment, and eventual happiness. Gratitude allows you to appreciate how far you've come, while an act of forgiveness gives you the fuel to rewrite history and defuse an unpleasant or embittering event. By doing this, you can actually transform bad memories into better ones.

One process that I find works is to face the memories head on and decatastrophize them. Let's say you've taken a bracelet your mother may have earmarked for your sister; your sister is upset that you've taken her inheritance and won't speak to you. Or suppose you keep falling off a diet and gaining back more weight. Your husband doesn't like how you look when you're overweight, and he rejects you sexually.

Ask yourself a number of leading questions about either of these events, such as

- What are the implications of your behavior in this event?
- Is it true that you took a bracelet you knew would not be left to you?
- Do you resent your sister because you feel your mother preferred her?
- What is the nature of your relationship with her?

- What does overeating do for you?
- Do you want your husband to accept you at any weight and resent him for not desiring you?
- Or have you gained weight because you don't want to have sex with him?
- Are you using your husband's responses to you as a recipe for completely letting go of your diet?

Should one incident really lead to estrangement from a sister or to divorce? Do you, above all, feel that you're a terrible person because you feel justified in your position? Do you fear you've somehow done great damage to a relationship? You've been through tough times with your sister and your husband. You've survived and recovered, and you can recover again. If your negative emotions trump the broadening, building, abiding but more fragile positive emotions, take charge.

There's power in positive emotions and a sense of helplessness in negative ones. You can't feel happy and helpless at the same time. Positive emotions can help undo negative emotions.

Of course, it's possible to be proud and satisfied about the past but sour or unhappy about the present and pessimistic about the future. These three attitudes and the feelings they invoke between time periods are not necessarily linked. So in what context does emotion drive thinking, and under what conditions does thinking drive emotion? Either one can ignite the other.

It's not uncommon for a blow to your ego to set off a crisis of confidence and therefore negative feelings. You lost track of time and were half an hour late picking your child up at school, and she was teary-eyed and worried about where you were. What sets it off is a comment, say, from your husband, who says, "What kind of mother are you, leaving a seven-year-old waiting in a schoolyard?"

Right then, you believe your husband's inference that you're a bad mother. But you would not admit to your husband how you feel. The consequence is that at dinnertime you snap at everyone in your family. You think, "How dare he think I'm a bad mother! I'll show him and do 'bad mother' things, so everyone will remember how I'm mostly good, but now they're not getting any of that goodness."

The present time doesn't feel good. You need to examine how you reached the argument with yourself to play out the "bad mother." What's the truth of the situation? You're a mostly good, attentive, and caring mother who sometimes makes mistakes. Although your daughter was scared, she was in a safe environment, since there was a supervised after-school game going on in the yard. It wasn't nice to make your daughter wait, but it wasn't done deliberately, and it was not a terrible act. Your husband hurt you by what he said, but he's not the final judge of who you are. Thus, forgive him and yourself for what happened, and experience the lightness of defused anger.

The human brain has evolved with great sophistication, and our faculty of using reason over emotion is pretty potent. Then there are exceptions. Some negative moods activate the brain's battle stations to give us the ammunition of *focus*—negativity or not, we can hone in on a problem-solving mode to eliminate what's wrong. This kind of problem solving works when the task requires critical thinking, such as taking an exam, doing your taxes, or stopping the roof from falling in. Being uptight or out-of-sorts may actually have a positive effect on your making more concrete decisions, like figuring something out what to do next.

In contrast to this, life tasks that call for creative, generous, and tolerant thinking, such as thinking of how to increase love or make a new career choice require a setting that will buoy your mood—music, sunshine, or an environment of happy people are helpful. Adults and children who put themselves in a good mood tend to select higher goals, perform better, and persist longer in a variety of tasks. And researchers on the subject have found that happy people even endure pain better and take more health and safety precautions.

EXPECTATIONS AND HAPPINESS

Happiness depends on what you say it is. However, what you want and how you expect it to come may have little in common. There are many women who talk about being unhappy when what they're really talking about is unrealistic expectations about what life is about.

I treat a number of women who tell me they want powerful, ambitious men and the material goods that go with his success. They also want these men to be loving, sweet-tempered, generous, and home every night by six for dinner. They don't understand how ambition works. A man with big plans for his future won't be home at the same time every night, never mind in time for a typical dinner hour. If he weren't driven, he wouldn't have power and all the status stuff that contributes to his appeal to some women. If he weren't ambitious, he'd be working nine-to-five and at the end of the day he'd be out the office door on a rocket.

A patient said to me on the subject, "I want a life like, say, Nancy Reagan or Hillary Clinton. Both women had powerful, successful husbands and both are known to be as ambitious as their husbands. These couples went on a ride to the top, relying on each other all the time. I want a relationship like that. Maybe not a politician, but a man in business, with the same kind of drive. Is this too much to expect?" No matter how we analyze them, no one really knows why these relationships work long-term, scandals or not. No one is really clear about what Mrs. Reagan and Mrs. Clinton expected from their husbands. Only the spoon knows what's in the pot.

Does this patient have what both Nancy Reagan and Hillary Clinton had to stay in their marriages with husbands who did not come home for dinner by six? In her case, to answer her question, it *is* too much to expect. Unrealistic expectations give you false impressions that you can get one side of the equation without the other. She wants the romance of power and the prosperity that goes with it. But what does she have to give, or give up, to get it? Does she even want to know?

When you hold on to unrealistic expectations, you want the goods, but not the responsibility for the package they come in. It's a nice dream to wish for your version of a business powerhouse, but what is your trade-off for having a relationship with a man who has little time for you? What can you contribute to his life? What about you makes you his right partner? A number of women want a successful man only to be well taken care of and don't want to give much in return. This dream is really about dependency, not being one-half of a team, shoulder-to-shoulder, making its mark in the world.

The issue of unrealistic expectations applies to what we want from others and what we want from things, too. Women spend billions of dollars on creams to look better, smoother, and younger. Those creams aren't going to make a real difference beyond plumping the wrinkles a little. They won't erase ten years in two weeks of applications. We want to lose ten pounds over a weekend, and keep it off. We expect the products to work, even if a more reasonable voice in our heads is saying they won't. We expect to achieve the end but do not want to do the long-term work.

Holding on to unrealistic expectations can only get you into trouble. You'll always be unhappy when you rely on miracles rather than your own energy, input, and sensibility.

We all grew up with expectations designed to help us fit into the society in which we live, and which were meant to make us happy. I'm sure your mother had an idea of what she expected for herself and for you. Mine did. My mother had a survival mentality that revolved around the basics—a man should have a steady job and bring home food. She never really gave life much thought beyond that for herself or for me. However, she wasn't satisfied with how she was taken care of by my father or stepfather, and she never defined her expectations for herself.

Unrealistic expectations should not be your measure for defining standards. You need to be reasonable, realistic, and give yourself enough latitude to make changes. Most of all, if you enter into a relationship with a man, be sure both of you have a consensus of definition about your expectations in a partner. What are the particulars, and can you or do you want to fulfill them? You have to say to a guy, "What do you expect from a wife?" and then ask yourself, "What do I expect from a husband?"

By not having a definition of expectations, you will continue to search for happiness without knowing what you're searching for or even if you've already got it, have been sleeping with it, eating with it, and looking at it every day. There's always the chance that you might define your expectations and not get what you want. However, you absolutely *won't* get what you want if you don't think it out. Some people are afraid to define what they want thinking that doing so will limit their possibilities. Instead of seeing a definition as culling the flock, their fear is that it will scare off a prospective husband and then, what if no one else comes along? This thinking gets you into trouble.

A patient who is now in her early sixties left her husband in the mid-1970s, believing she could do better for herself than Hal. Pam's expectations were raised by listening to speakers in the woman's movement at the time. She says they made her feel there was something more out there than a nice-enough husband. There wasn't. She expected a better life, a better career, and a better man, one who'd have more money, love her differently, and would be more reliable. Pam is kicking herself around the block now, wishing she'd never left Hal. In making her decision to leave, the possibility never occurred to her that she might end up alone.

Expectations are ideas and ideas are under your voluntary control. Make the effort to understand your expectations and to change them as you need to. When you do, your level of happiness is likely to increase in a lasting manner.

WHAT MAKES YOU HAPPY?

It's important to take a tally every once in a while of what is and isn't of great value in your life. Write a couple of sentences that sum them up, whether it is your love life, family, children, finances, work, play, friends, health, your sense of self, and your community. Make a trajectory of where you want to be, where you are, and how you might make your life better.

What would make you happier? Here are some ideas to ponder.

A rich and fulfilling social life markedly differentiates the very happy from the unhappy people. Very happy people spend the least time alone; they have more friends, both casual and close ones. They are more likely to be paired in a couple and more involved in group activities than unhappy people. Happy people tend to be altruistic, display more empathy, and are willing to donate more money to those in need.

One of the ways to savor good things is to share it with others. Do not hesitate to say positive things to yourself and to others. Sharpen your focus on what you are enjoying, and get totally immersed in it. Savor your experiences, and luxuriate in the moment. Be mindful of how you experience life, being sure not to simply act or interact automatically without paying attention. Take a stale situation and make it fresh by looking for something new or different in it.

The strident philosophy of "looking out for number one" is more characteristic of a sad personality than one with inner strength and smarts. Developing more positive emotion builds friendship, love, better physical health, and greater achievement.

FINALLY . . . PERMIT YOURSELF TO EXPERIENCE JOY

A joyous spirit finds its meaning in small things. There is the joy of doing for others, of doing a good job just for the pleasure of it, the joy of seeing the good in others and praising it. The ultimate joy is to believe in yourself and appreciate the great gift of life.

Here are a few questions to ask yourself about the meaning of happiness for you:

- How do you define happiness?
- Who do you really see as being responsible for your happiness?
- When is the last time you remember feeling happy?
- What was going on around you?
- Is it difficult or even impossible for you to see a good result or a happy ending? Do you always think negatively, believing you are warding off "the evil eye"?
- Are you typically more aware of the negative than the positive events around you?
- If you describe yourself as pessimistic, how does thinking negatively keep you in the past?
- Can you think of something good that happened to you today?

- Are you willing to see positive things around you?
- Could you get up every morning and commit to making it a good day?
- Can you concentrate on today and let yesterday go?
- What are you grateful for?
- Are your expectations of others realistic?
- Can you get out of your own orbit and do things for others?
- Were you raised to be agreeable at all costs and to sacrifice your feelings for others?
- Would you say you are never happy and worry all the time?
- Can you recall a moment when you felt happy and never wanted it to end?
- Which of your signature strengths, such as courage or kindness, make you and others happy?
- Can you tell whether you are giving yourself positive or negative messages? Are you willing to say more positive words to yourself?
- Is rejection hard for you to take, or do you recover and move on easily?
- If your answer to the previous question is yes, what would it take for you to move on?

~9~

MAKING LIFE MATTER NOW

Opening the Present of Your Life

A friend and I were discussing "Portraits in Grief," *The New York Times* series that profiled each of the World Trade Center victims. Other than trying to comprehend the diabolical motive for the disaster that buried these people before their time, what struck us was the number of times we'd read phrases in these biographies like, "She could have been . . ." "He wanted to be . . ." "Her dream was to . . ." These were words about *lost possibilities*, heart-wrenching to read.

If the September 11th events put an end to America's complacency as an invulnerable power, so did that terrorist ambush make every one of us breathe a heavy sigh and think, "That could have been me—and I'm lucky to be alive." Because of this life-changing day in September, we want *more* of life itself and we want that life to be a better one. But how to get it?

I hear a new sense of urgency when patients, friends, or audiences at one of my lectures tell me how they're unable to move their lives forward. The unthinkable possibility of being blown away and never knowing "what could have been" foreshadow their concerns. So many women talk about how to heal relationships or make healthy, longstanding connections to others. They ask me what to do first and how to do it.

As the mantra of the transcendental generation in the 1970s was, "Be here now," my answer to them, and to you, would be, "*Take it from here*"—a mantra for the twenty-first century.

What's happening worldwide is a reflection, of sorts, of what can happen to us individually. The September 11th disaster put a really fine point on this. Now we need to reassess the meaning of life and its finiteness. Since the world has changed forever, it's even more important to be clear about who you are, what you value, the kind of people you want to surround yourself with, and what life path you want to follow.

Only you can create the true portrait of your life, with color, texture, feeling, spontaneity, and joy. The truth remains that *you* control what you think, what you say, how you feel, and how you behave. Taking control takes courage, but it's the only way to be true to yourself and prevent destructive forces from steering you off your course. Since life is short, you cannot let others keep time for you—or give your life over to procrastination.

The greatest gift you will ever have is your life, and the second greatest gift—which you give yourself—is courage to live it to the fullest. Time goes by quickly, and you cannot take it for granted. Appreciate how far you have come, and give yourself the gift of discovering how far you can yet go.

THE PRESENT OF YOUR LIFE!

Opening the "present of your life" is a concept with a double meaning relating to time and to the gift of life. First, it's meant to be a catch-phrase that helps you move your agenda up from the vague foreseeable future to the immediate moment. Think about where you want to be, what's missing, how you can get it, and what you need to change about yourself so you can act *now*. By bringing your life *into the present*, you break out of the cocoon of past mistakes that keeps you in the same psychological place.

My meaning also suggests that the "present" of your life is a gift that continues to evolve. This is not the kind of gift you put on a shelf in the back of a closet, but one you take out, cherish, and make to fit you. This is a gift that identifies you as you—a self that continues on. What is more blessed than a life that's capable of becoming more?

When you open the present of your life as a grown-up, you find in it reliability, stability, passion, and honest affection where you once found extreme peaks and valleys of emotion. You can be true to yourself and think, "I don't like this about myself, but I'm clear about who I am. I can give this up or try that without having to tell everyone what I'm doing." Do you still do what's wrong for you, knowing the consequences, or are you wiser?

My friend Claudia stopped smoking, finally and forever, after twelve tries over twelve years. She'd started smoking in high school, when she was sixteen years old, hanging out with her older brother's garage band, most of them smokers, and their girlfriends, most of them smokers, too.

When she was twenty-eight years old, Claudia was up to two packs a day and eager to stop. Over the next dozen years, she would stop smoking during the summers but resume in the fall. She began going for serious help: she went to a group at the American Cancer Society, to the Seventh Day Adventists' five-day program, to Smoke Enders, to a hypnotist to learn self-hypnosis, to an acupuncturist who put a "staple" in her ear. Claudia could not stay away from cigarettes for more than six months. Then came the turning point.

When she was forty, she and her husband still wanted a child and Claudia was not getting pregnant. She told me, "I knew smoking could be factor, and I decided to do everything possible to conceive. I literally stopped smoking the moment I made the decision. I had been through so many programs, I knew what I'd go through physically and mentally—I had the chemistry of nicotine addiction down pat. It's just seventy-two hours of misery, then the stuff is out of your system. After that, it's all in your head. For the next week, I was obsessed about *not* smoking, and kept wanting to stop people in the street and say something ridiculous, like, 'Do you notice that *I'm not smoking?*' Eventually, I lost all interest in cigarettes and haven't had a single puff since."

Claudia's experience illustrates one way to answer the questions of (1) how do you open the present of your life, and (2) how do you stop the past from running out in front of you and becoming your future? Claudia was able to change because *what she wanted right then*—a baby—*was more important than what she had*—an addiction that could prevent her from achieving her goal. "If I really want something, I lay out what I have to do, step by step," she said.

Claudia's story sounds very simple: pick your destination, travel in a straight line from point A to point B, and plant your flag in triumph on the hill. Hers is a wonderful story because it's the story all of us are familiar with—how we can keep on trying. Maybe it's trying to lose weight, trying to control your temper, trying to call your estranged father, trying to get off the couch and get a job, trying to find a life mate.

Claudia tried to stop smoking, until she did. "I never felt like a failure when I couldn't stay off cigarettes. I just waited until I was ready and tried again." This is a very positive attitude to have about yourself and how you achieve your goals, the kind of attitude that can apply to any arena in your life. Research shows that Claudia's approach has merit: the more you keep trying, the greater your chances for success.

There are no magic words that will make your problems disappear or endow you with resistance to your weaknesses and the lure of temptation. I wish I could say that taking *vows* to change self-sabotaging patterns are enough, but they usually don't work. Promises are made with good intentions, but they can be rationalized away or put off. Maybe you vow to stand up for yourself in an abusive relationship, or end a hedonistic lifestyle, or say, "I love you," to your parents, but you never get around to it. Rely on vows as being magic words and you may never change and improve.

Transformation occurs when you build "emotional muscle"— making actual attempts to change. It took Claudia all those years to stop smoking, but each time she tried she was getting an "emotional workout," gaining a little more strength to quit. It's not unlike weight training at a gym. You start with a one-pound weight, and it may feel a little unwieldy, but you keep flexing and strengthening. A few weeks later, you're pumping with five-pound weights, then fifteen-pounders, and so on. In terms of psychological change, each emotional pump will eventually give you more power to change. You are stronger and able to say, "*This* is not important to me, but *that* is."

⁓

Since women in this twenty-first century have so many choices, we can no longer blame spouses, parents, disadvantaged or privileged childhoods, or corporate machinery for personal limitations. We're pretty much responsible for where we've arrived in life so far. The present of every woman's life—what matters now—is not only in exploring talents and abilities in the workplace, but in civilizing men and society, being standard bearers, raising daughters who respect themselves and who are not sexually active at fourteen years old—and raising sons who are not materialistic or overbearing and who respect women.

I recently took a cab from the airport in Detroit and got into a fascinating conversation with the cabdriver, a twenty-one-year-old

African American man with dreams and levelheaded insights. He told me a little about his life and his observation that men didn't like women. I asked him why he thought that was the case. He told me, "When you're a kid and your father's left, like my father did, you go through stuff. Maybe your mother beats up on you and says, 'Your father doesn't care about you,' and 'You're just like your father,' and what does she need you for? and you grow up *not* liking women. Then sometimes," he added, "you get a stepmother and the relationship goes wrong between her and your father. Now *she's* saying the same thing to you."

I asked him what he thought women could do to be better mothers. This young man with aspirations to work in the movie business seemed to have his past in perspective and his anger in check. He said, "Women have to learn how to pick men who are going to be hangin' around them a while so that kids like me don't have to grow up hearin' that bad stuff."

How simply and movingly this young man stated how he felt. In a few words, he described everything that happens to children when parents do not care about each other. My own father left, and I know how it feels when a mother, in her frustration with her life's circumstances, lashes out at her child. I know the rejection, first hand, of attempting to have a relationship with a stepparent who isn't interested in you. What probably saved me from the kind of psychological damage that the cabdriver suffered was that I wasn't a boy. But my mother also said the same kind of hurtful words, like, "Your father doesn't want you or care about you!" While her remarks didn't poison me against men, it did make me fear their having any control over me. I needed to be sure that I was never in my mother's shoes—dependent on men who weren't there for me. Fortunately, I was able to choose a man who could be depended upon. This young cabdriver also survived his early life and probably will do what his father did not do for him—be there for a woman and for his kids. He's a grown-up, at twenty-one.

WHAT IS YOUR LEGACY?

When we think about legacies, what comes to mind is usually the passing down of property from one person to the next—anything from real estate to a box of old photographs. Actual inherited property can make you feel sentimental, reconnected to someone who's gone, or, if you feel left out or shortchanged, then that legacy is resentment. Legacies also bring up your heritage or genealogy, and you can even easily track your relatives' immigration records at sites like the Ellis Island Web site. There is yet another legacy to pass down to your children, something you might want to begin considering: an ethical will.

An ethical will asks that you consider what you want to leave to your children, not in terms of material things or romantic history, but as *accumulated life wisdom*. It is a diary of decisions, right and wrong—a continuing commentary on the ethics by which you live. Making an ethical will provides you with an opportunity to see where you've been and where you are. The maturity you reach in the journey of your life makes up that wisdom. One of the greatest legacies you can leave is a positive impact on another's person life, an impact that will carry on. One of the greatest compliments you could receive is hearing one of your children say, "What would Mom say in a situation like this?" or, "Mom would know what to do now." It's even nice to hear, "My mother had the best recipe for that."

My daughter Sharon told me that she's tried about a dozen versions of stuffed cabbage, which her family loves, and she keeps going back to my recipe. "Make sure you give me your stuffed cabbage recipe," she said each time I served it. Over the years, I've made little changes in the seasonings or proportion of ingredients until I settled on what I liked best, which is now part of a family tradition. This makes me feel good. I want my family to have the best of me, whether in regard to recipes or wisdom.

The same is true for you. You hope your children will hear your voice in their heads asking, "Will this make your life better?" when they are about to make an important decision.

What wisdom have you gained and wish to pass on? What makes up your ethical will? Be there for your kids. Write down what you want to say to them, or tape it.

Share What You Know with Others

Sharing knowledge is not just a generous act; in these times, it's a moral obligation! Giving knowledge to your children inspires you to learn more, expand your ideas, shift your focus from yourself to them, develop patience, and learn the value of teaching. If sharing what you know is unselfish, then hoarding it isolates you. And when you share knowledge, you get knowledge.

When you take others into your circle of wisdom, you grow and evolve spiritually and help others do the same. This sharing is part of the basic human creative process. By imparting guidance or wisdom based on your accumulated knowledge and breadth of experience, you can save others from potential disasters. As you've been advised or given a leg up by someone who believed in you, you have an obligation to do the same for others. You need not expect those you teach to follow you blindly, but to consider your information and test it.

Experience Awe and Take in the Greatness of the World

You don't have to be religious to have a spiritual attachment to nature and see the beauty in the world. Yes, it's a tough, baffling, and often unfair place. But your children need to know that to love life and find fulfillment, they must also appreciate another plane on which life takes place, a transcendental plane.

This could be part of your spiritual legacy to them—the suggestion that they remain fascinated with life, allow themself to experience awe, and never get bored. Boredom is about seeing scarcity in the bounty around you. A certain form of laziness, boredom is a state that demands others entertain you and show you something different. In fact, boredom is a symptom of resistance to taking control of your life.

When you connect with nature, you again connect with something greater than yourself. The key is to never be satisfied with what you know and know of, but to search for peak experiences, information, and delight in the world.

The Legacy of Maturity

The theme of this book is growing up so that you can open the door to the best part of you. I don't know of a better entry in an ethical will than stressing to your children that maturity is worth striving for. Maturity, remember, is not assigned to any age. It means becoming an emotionally generous person—forgiving, positive, capable of creating boundaries in relationships without damaging other people. It means coming to terms with the finiteness of life and ending it well. Maturity helps you make choices about your life that will allow you to experience your future with excitement and enthusiasm, even if you've never had those feelings before.

Maturity will arrive through the completion of adult developmental tasks—a result of hard work and insight into what is truly important in life. It will give your children a new sense of power and accomplishment. They'll know they've "earned their stripes" as opposed to automatically feeling entitled to respect, love, and status.

Understand More About Yourself Through Your Children and Let Them Know It

After thirty years of practice, I'm seeing more mothers and adult daughters in my office whose issues are not about problems with spouses, or an inability to find love. These days, I'm seeing more and more women who are trying to repair family relationships. Among them are mothers who can no longer tolerate the fact that their children do not speak to one another, or that they never see their grandchildren. Some women need their husbands to communicate with their own mothers because they find them too demanding, resolute, or guilt-making to contend with. There are mothers who insist on ruling their married children's families, yet they don't understand why they're left out of celebrations.

There are also mothers who do a great job in raising a great daughter, but still don't want her to follow her own path. And then, thankfully, some see the light. That daughters should become different from their mothers is hardly unusual. What's interesting is when a mother does not see how very alike her daughter is to herself, but in another incarnation. I'll give you a quick example of this.

My hairdresser and friend, Sabah, has one of the most fabulous daughters I've ever met. Sabah came to this country from Lebanon as an immigrant with her husband and children. She worked at and then managed a popular salon. She was widowed before her daughter was admitted to medical school. One of Sabah's clients, who loved and admired her, put together a scholarship fund with other clients to help pay for Michelene's schooling. Michelene ultimately graduated and became an internist. She recently married a lovely man, an engineer, and then decided to take six months off to travel the world with him, backpacking all the way. Sabah was not happy. "She should be working at this stage of her life, not running around the world," she said.

With her strong work ethic, Sabah felt that she'd come to this country with nothing, and that her daughter was making light of everything that had been given to her. Not only had Sabah invested in her future and daughter's education, but so had her friends and clients.

While Sabah felt hurt by her daughter's decision to take a break from her career at this particular point, I concurred with Michelene's decision. Of all the times to explore the world with a new love, *this was the moment*. She'll probably not have a chance to take six months off again for a very long time. About two weeks after Michelene left on her journey, Sabah told me she'd had a revelation: "I've been thinking about what Michelene is doing, and it really isn't very different from the way I lived when I was first married," she said. "My husband and I left Lebanon and took a chance. We lived in Canada, then traveled around Europe and lived in London for a while. I thought to myself, isn't that interesting that I forgot what it was like to have that young blood, to be that person. She's just like me. I wanted to explore the world, too."

All of a sudden, your life makes sense, your daughter's life makes sense, and you know your legacy lives on.

FINALLY . . .

The bottom line is that life is short, and *change is choice*. You can either hang on to destructive patterns that don't work, or go through a brief period of discomfort that finally allows you the joy of growing up.

I hope that this book has helped you gain greater insight into yourself. In an unpredictable world, don't lose the ability to be grateful for what you have. Don't make the mistake of noticing only what's *missing*. Count your blessings! And keep putting one foot in front of the other to move forward. When you grow up, you'll like yourself a lot better, and you'll like your life a lot better, too.

Here are the final questions to ask yourself about living your life now:

- Before making a decision, do you ask yourself, "Is this right or good for me?"
- What regrets, if any, do you have about your life?
- What can you do about acting on those regrets?
- Since you can't change what's occurred, can you let go of hurtful events?
- Are you willing to move forward?
- Have you learned from past mistakes?
- What are the values, standards, and slogans you are leaving to your children?
- What legacy would you like to leave?

As this book ends, let me leave you with a final thought: If you're the same person at fifty years old as you were at twenty, you've wasted thirty years! Even if this is the case, start now to "Take it from here."